Preserved Foods and Sweetmeats

Preserved Foods and Sweetmeats

A HANDBOOK OF ALL
The Process for the Preservation of Flesh, Fruits and Vegetables, and for the Preparation of Dried Fruits, Dried Vegetables, Marmalades, Fruit-Syrups, and Fermented Beverages, and of All Kinds of Candies, Candied Fruit, Sweetmeats, Rocks, Drops, Dragées, Pralines etc.

— 3rd Revised and Enlarged edn —

by
A. Hausner

2012
BIOTECH BOOKS
Delhi - 110 035

ISBN 81-7622-143-0

Original Title: The Manufacture of Preserved Foods and Sweetmeats

Published by : **BIOTECH BOOKS**
1123/74, Tri Nagar,
Delhi - 110 035
Phone: 27382765
e-mail: biotechbooks@yahoo.co.in

Showroom : 4762-63/23, Ansari Road, Darya Ganj,
New Delhi - 110 002
Phone: 23245578, 23244987

Laser Typesetting : **Classic Computer Services**
Delhi - 110 035

Printed at : **Chawla Offset Printers**
Delhi - 110 052

PRINTED IN INDIA

Preface

In preparing this, the third edition of my work, I have subjected it to a thorough revision, and have weeded out everything that has become antiquated.

In view of the great progress that has of late been made in the preservation of animal food in a fresh state, it has appeared to me essential to give much more space to the portion of the book referring to these processes, and to rewrite it for the most part. The same attention has been given in the case of all progress in the art of making preserved foods of all kinds.

As I have already stated in the preface to the second edition, my aim has been to make my book not merely a means of studying the theory of the preserving art, but a guide to its practical application to every class of food. In as much as the preparation of sweetmeats stands in the very closest relationship to the art of preserving edible articles, often, in fact, merely consisting in such preservation, a second part has been added, so that the work now includes everything which is of interest to those whose business lies is these directions.

If I have attained my object of writing a really practical book, I shall be richly rewarded for my trouble. I shall be very grateful to any expert who will supply me with anything from the treasures of his practical experience which will increase the value of my next edition.

A. Hausner

Contents

Part II
THE MANUFACTURE OF SWEETMEATS

Part I

Manufacture of Preserved Foods

Chapter 1
Introduction

Nearly all kinds of food used by man have the property of soon becoming uneatable. In large towns with a well-organised system of trade, and where the consumption is rapid and keeps pace with the supply of fresh food, this fact is not of very great consequence, and there is little fear of food going bad, even in the summer.

In spite of, and also in the presence of, these favourable conditions, the necessity has arisen of having a constant daily supply at a given place of articles either not produced there at all, or only produced there at certain seasons of the year. This is the case with vegetables, for example, some descriptions of which cannot be obtained fresh in the winter; and with the products of the sea in towns far from the coast; and especially in cold countries with the products of warmer climates.

The human race have, therefore, been induced to attempt to preserve food, and to assure its keeping properties for a series of years even. Preserved foods of many different kinds, both animal and vegetable, have resulted from these attempts. The term "preserves" is of course, in England at least, restricted to sweetmeats.[1]

The preservation of food is now in many countries a gigantic industry. It is unfortunate that in Germany the industry is in a more backward state than in the great maritime nations, where foods are preserved on a vast scale. Even the provisioning of their ships affords them an outlet for enormous quantities of these products.

That the manufacture of preserved foods has attained dimensions too great for any one man to review thoroughly is beyond a doubt. It actually exceeds its power of distribution, in spite of the development of steam transport. This makes itself felt in the supply of large cities with articles which can only be produced in comparatively small quantities or at certain times of the year. Take for example milk, which will not bear a long journey, and eggs, which outside rural districts can only be had really fresh at certain seasons.

In thinly populated country neighbourhoods large quantities of milk are produced, which would be a source of greater profit if they could be sent in a natural state to the large towns than in the form of butter and cheese.

Of still greater importance is the preservation of meat. Here the price is not entirely dependent on mercantile considerations, but, independently also of the political importance of the trade in time of war, is largely influenced by sanitary regulations. If, for example, rinderpest or other cattle disease breaks out in a country, the sanitary authorities stop all export of meat from it for the time being, with the natural result that the countries normally drawing their supplies from the infected area experience a considerable rise in prices. Even independently of great calamities, moreover, many little things show how important is the trade in preserved foods. It is notorious that during a long severe winter the price of eggs rises greatly, and the demand can scarcely be met. If it were a common practice to preserve

[1] The translator finds it necessary to use the name of the particular article of food, with the adjective "preserved" before it. In Germany the collective term "*Conserve*" is used for preserved foods of all kinds.

eggs whole, or the white and yolk separately, this would not be the case.

The inhabitants of a large town require the service of a very extended area of food-production, and the cost of transport has to be added to the selling price of the food. When it is a question of foods which in certain districts can only be produced in comparatively small quantities, and are, moreover, very liable to go bad, such as milk, eggs, butter, ripe fruits etc. we not only find that their prices vary extremely in large towns, but that they are usually of decidedly inferior quality, or may be utterly ruined by adulterations intended to increase the supply apparently available.

We are here alluding chiefly to two articles of daily consumption: milk and butter. The former is diluted by fraudulent dealers with water, or mixed with antiseptics, which may produce serious results in delicate stomachs. The consumers of butter are exposed to still greater frauds; for while the milk-buyer does get milk, even if it is adulterated, the would-be purchaser of butter often gets an article which, if it resembles butter in appearance, smell, and taste, has an origin absolutely distinct from that of the genuine article.[1]

If these foods which are so liable to putrefaction were used exclusively in a preserved form, a double advantage would be secured; for not only would they be sold in an unadulterated condition, but they would always be procurable at the same price, for the producing district could be hundreds of miles from the place where the food was consumed.

We may mention, as two brilliant examples of world-wide success achieved by preserved food, Liebig's extract of beef, and condensed milk.

The meat-extract is prepared at Fray Bentos, in South America, from meat which is there almost without value, the animals being slaughtered for their skin and fat, and its use has spread over the whole earth. What was necessary, however, to establish such a manufacture in those distant countries was English capital, the employment of which for the purpose could only be secured by the influence of a learned man of the calibre of Liebig, whose claim to greatness might well, if it were necessary, rest on his meat-extract alone.

---

[1] Butter comes from the cow, margarine often from the bull.–Tr.

The case of condensed milk is very similar. The Alpine lands of Southern Europe–Switzerland, Tyrol, Salzburg, and the Steiermark–produce such huge quantities of milk that the conversion of it into cheese is a source of little profit. The dairies that convert all their product into condensed milk obtain on the other hand much larger returns; and we are of opinion that if the condensed milk manufacture was carried to a sufficient extent in those countries, the difficulty of milk supply, which is a chronic evil in large towns, and the troubles with which the sanitary authorities attempt in vain to cope, would disappear at once and altogether.

We have to congratulate ourselves on the great progress of the food-preserving art of late years. At the Vienna Exhibition of 1873, and at those at Paris in 1878 and 1889, we met with preserved Australian mutton, and we cannot refrain from observing that it is in nearly every case that practical race, the English, who have taken this industry in hand. This fact alone guarantees that favourable results must ensue from the manufacture of preserved food if rightly carried out. The exhibits at Paris in 1878 showed marked improvement on those at Vienna only five years before.

The large towns and thickly peopled centres generally form, of course, the greatest sources of demand for preserved foods; that is, all countries and places where agriculture is the smaller and manufacture the larger part of the occupation of the people. We must also put in the same category all states which are compelled to import food largely and often from very distant countries. That this is exactly the position of the majority of European countries is a well-known fact. Even those which must certainly be characterised as agricultural states cannot usually feed themselves entirely, and must therefore import food-stuffs from abroad.

It is hardly necessary to mention the importance of preserved foods to armies in the field, for the provisioning of fortified places, and for voyages by sea. In former times the sickness resulting on long voyages from the want of fresh meat and vegetables was appalling, but it has almost disappeared with the improvement in food-preservation. Scurvy is now little more than a name of purely historical interest.

Expeditions intended to be sent out on voyages of discovery had often to be abandoned on account of the impossibility of provisioning them. They can now carry an ample supply of preserved foods for use when fresh meat and vegetables cannot be obtained.

Our Age, which demands much more labour from the individual than was formerly the case, has written the principle of the division of labour upon its banner. But in connection with the weighty question of nourishment, which lies at the foundation of all human work, we have not made corresponding progress. When we consider the expenditure of labour and time in every household in the preparation of meals, and what vast quantities of food-refuse has to be got rid of even by the most thrifty housewife, we are filled with astonishment that preserved foods are not more extensively used in home-life.

We think, however, that the prophecy that in the near future matters will be greatly altered in this direction is no idle dream. We believe that cooking will be practised in the household only to a comparatively limited extent, and that most of the food will be bought ready cooked in a preserved form, and requiring only very slight preparation before serving.

We conclude this introduction by repeating that the food-preserving industry is still awaiting fuller development, and is destined to reach colossal magnitude, which will surpass anything we can imagine. That it has not made even further progress than has been realised is due, we think, chiefly to the food-preservers themselves, who in many cases have embarked in the business with insufficient knowledge, and created prejudice by putting unsatisfactory articles upon the market. With proper knowledge and due observance of known precautions such results can be obviated.

Most foods are bodies which very soon go bad, many of them deteriorating in a few hours, others in a few days. A few, especially fruits, can be kept good for months. As the chief object of the food-preserver is to enable it to be kept for unlimited time in its original condition, we must consider fully the natural processes of putrefaction before we can expect to find out how to prevent them.

Chapter 2

The Causes of the Putrefaction of Food

All vegetable and animal substances which we use as food are liable to putrefaction. We usually distinguish three varieties of change: fermentation, mould, and putrefaction.

Fermentation usually means a change accompanied by the evolution of gas, but not gas of an evil-smelling kind. The best-known example of it is the production of alcohol from sugar, a change which, although it is not putrefactive, is the first step in that direction.

The turning sour of wine and beer, of fruit-juices, milk, and many other changes must be included among fermentation processes. These changes, which are the preliminary processes to putrefaction, are of special importance. It must be mentioned that we are not in a position exactly to define fermentation. Very many chemists understand by the term all so-called spontaneous changes. In this sense all the three processes above enumerated are fermentation, just as much as alcoholic fermentation itself.

Coming next to putrefaction, we find the idea associated with the development of a foul smell, caused by the production of certain volatile substances. Good examples are afforded by the changes undergone by meat or eggs under ordinary circumstances.

Mould is characterized by gradual change unaccompanied by evolution of gas or the production of evil odours. Vinegar, for example, gradually loses its sour taste on keeping, and cheese, stored for very long periods in a dry place, becomes ultimately converted into a white dust.

All these changes are influenced by three factors which lie at the root of each of them, and which the preserver has to contend against. These influences rarely need purposeful action to bring them into play, as they are almost invariably at hand from natural causes. They are as follow:

First, the presence of a certain amount of water. This is a necessary condition of decomposition, so that we find in the removal of it one of the simplest and surest means of preservation. The second, which is just as essential a condition as the first, is the presence of a certain amount of heat. Except within certain limits of temperature no change can take place. The change, however, which we have described as mould may be the result of purely chemical action, and hence for it the temperature limits are much wider than for either fermentation or putrefaction. We have here another means of food-preservation, and it is, in general, enough to get rid of one only of the three conditions in order to prevent the food from changing. The third condition, which is in many cases absolutely necessary for change, is the presence of air. This presence, be it observed, never hinders change, and in the great majority of cases favours it. We know, however, of a very large number of processes which can be reckoned as fermentative which go on perfectly well without any air being present. In some cases, therefore, the exclusion of air is an effectual preservative method, and in others it is of no use whatever.

When we consider the chemical changes in general which result in food going bad, we find that the process is always a deterioration from bodies of more to bodies of less complex constitution. The original chemical compounds pass step by step to simple inorganic substances. In many cases an invariable sequence of change has been proved to exist.

Before proceeding to the processes taking place during fermentation and putrefaction, we must become acquainted with the chemical composition of unchanged food, and this obviously necessary preliminary will occupy our next chapter.

Chapter 3
The Chemical Composition of Foods

All known bodies are either elements or compounds. By elements the chemist means substances which cannot be decomposed by any known means, and which must therefore be considered as the simple bases of the compounds. We know at present more than seventy elements, many of which, however, are very rare, and have at present only a scientific interest. The number of those of universal importance, owing to their wide distribution and the immense number of substances, both mineral and occurring, in the bodies of animals and plants of which they form part, is about twenty.

When we turn to the compounds occurring in plants and animals only, we find that there is an enormous number of them, but they are constituted by a small number of elements and owe their great variety to the different proportions in which they contain these elements.

There are four principal elements of which organic matter is built up. These have therefore been called the organic elements, although the expression is entirely unjustifiable, inasmuch as although we always meet with them in organic matter, other elements also occur, although in smaller quantities. These elements are, however, of not the less importance for that, as many compounds cannot exist without them. With this before us, however, we can use the expression, and we find that the organic elements are as follow:

Carbon

This occurs in a pure state in nature under the various forms of graphite, diamond, and ordinary charcoal. Every substance produced by vital action, whether in a plant or animal body, contains carbon.

Hydrogen

This is a very light combustible gas, which occurs in water, and in very many organic substances.

Oxygen

This is one of the most widely distributed elements on the earth. In combination with hydrogen it forms water, it occurs in the free state in the atmosphere, and its very notable property is its great tendency to combine with other elements. The majority of plant and animal substances contain oxygen.

Nitrogen

This is a constituent of the air, of many minerals, and of a large number of organic substances. In contrast to oxygen it has very little tendency to enter into combination, and only does so with difficulty and under special circumstances.

Although these four elements constitute a very large number of the substances we meet with in the bodies of animals and plants, a few more must be mentioned which enter into the composition of a great many such bodies, although in smaller quantities than the four.

Sulphur and Phosphorus

The chief of these additional elements are sulphur and phosphorus. Pure sulphur is a crystalline body of characteristic yellow colour, which burns in the air with a suffocating smell, and has much resemblance to oxygen in its chemical properties. Sulphur occurs free in nature, and also combined in minerals, and in many bodies of organic origin. Pure phosphorus is a colourless, crystalline, and particularly poisonous substance which has a very great affinity for other bodies. Its affinity for oxygen, for example, is so great that it ignites spontaneously in the air. It will easily be inferred that phosphorus is never found in nature in the free state, but only in combination.

If we burn any constituent of an animal or vegetable body, a certain amount of incombustible residue remains which is known as the "ash." Little attention was at one time paid to this, and people even went so far as to consider it as something quite accidental, on account of its small quantity. Now, however, the progress of science has taught us that the bodies left in the ash are just as essential to the existence of the organisms as any one of the four elements which form the greatest proportion of them.

We find in the ash all those substances which are not volatile at the temperature produced by the combustion. They consist chiefly of metallic salts, such as carbonates, phosphates, and sulphates, and in most cases chlorides, potassium, sodium, magnesium, calcium, iron, and manganese.

The bodies above named–carbon, hydrogen, oxygen, nitrogen, sulphur, phosphorus, and silicon, together with the bodies of the ash, are the constituents of all animal and vegetable bodies.

The variety of these bodies is thus explained in chemistry. The compounds are formed by the union of two or more atoms (or very minute particles of the element, which are incapable of subdivision) combining, and so forming the molecule, or the smallest possible quantity of the compound.

If we pay no attention to the magnitude of the molecules, but only to the elements they contain, we shall find that all products of the animal and vegetable kingdoms can be grouped, as we will now briefly describe.

Compounds of carbon and oxygen alone are probably, when they occur among the constituents of an animal or vegetable body, chiefly products of putrefaction. Hydrocarbons (compounds of carbon with hydrogen only) occur in huge quantities in many plants, and constitute most of those volatile and usually strongly smelling bodies which we call essential oils. Turpentine may be taken as the representative of this group.

Ternary compounds (carbon, hydrogen, and oxygen) are abundant both in animals and in plants. The various kinds of sugar and gums, cellulose, the organic acids (*e.g.*, tartaric and malic acids), and all fats belong to this group, of which we have indicated only the most important members. These ternary compounds, together with others containing nitrogen, as well as carbon, hydrogen, and oxygen, form the second important group of organic bodies. The nitrogenous bodies include gluten, albumen, the chief constituents of flesh, and many others.

Many of these compounds always contain sulphur or phosphorus. Bodies which contain either or both of these elements in addition to the four chief organic elements must be made into a special sub-group, which includes egg-albumen and nerve-matter.

Chapter 4

The Products of Decomposition

If we abandon an organic body to decomposition, the processes gone through depend on the amount of nitrogen in the body, and as to whether or not air has access to it. But the final result is always a substance of very simple constitution.

The carbon of organic bodies becomes either carbonic acid or hydrocarbons. If enough oxygen is present, we get carbon dioxide CO_2 (*i.e.*, one atom of carbon combined with two atoms of oxygen), which combines with water to form carbonic acid. Pure carbonic acid is a colourless heavy gas of a weak, pleasantly acid taste, which when taken into the stomach, as in soda water or effervescent wine, is harmless, but is poisonous if inhaled into the lungs. In many cases the putrefaction takes the course of oxidising the carbon of one compound to carbonic acid at the expense of the oxygen of another and more complex substance, which is thus left poorer in oxygen. In ordinary language, putrefactive processes consisting largely in the production of carbonic acid, are those understood in the narrower sense of the term fermentation.

All decompositions in which sugar is converted into alcohol and carbonic acid (spirituous fermentation), and the changes in wood on long exposure to damp air, are of this nature.

If the carbon does not meet with enough oxygen it combines with hydrogen, forming for the most part gaseous compounds which are in some cases odourless, but which sometimes possess a very disagreeable smell. To these is due in part the odious stench which is developed by putrefying matter.

As an example of the product of this sort of decomposition, we may mention marsh gas, which rises in numerous bubbles when we stir up the bottom of a ditch in which the leaves of trees are putrefying. While the leaves which lie in the air gradually rot away, their carbon forming carbonic acid as it comes into contact with abundance of oxygen, the immersed leaves are shut off from oxygen and their carbon combines with hydrogen instead.

If an organic body contains nitrogen, that element combines during decomposition with hydrogen, forming ammonia, NH_3 (three atoms of hydrogen combined with one of nitrogen). This is an invisible gas of a sharp smell, which provokes tears. The suffocating smell of putrid urine is caused by the evolution of ammonia.

If an organic body contains sulphur, this also combines with hydrogen, forming sulphuretted hydrogen (H_2S), a gas with the repulsive odour of rotten eggs. Phosphorus, which is present in many animal substances, such as nerve-matter, also probably combines with hydrogen during decomposition.

With regard to the hydrogen of the organic matter, it combines, as we have seen, partly with carbon, nitrogen, or sulphur, but in the presence of abundance of oxygen, it unites with that element, forming water.

Carbonic acid, water, hydrocarbons, ammonia, and sulphuretted hydrogen are thus the final products of the shorter or longer series of chemical changes involved in putrefaction.

In ordinary language we call those actions which result in the formation of carbonic acid and water fermentation, and those producing large quantities of evil-smelling hydrocarbons, ammonia, and sulphuretted hydrogen, putrefaction. Grape juice left to itself ferments, an egg putrefies.

From a chemical point of view these ideas are wrong, for we are acquainted with fermentations unattended with any evolution of gas. The formation of vinegar from spirit of wine is a case in point. People have, however, become so accustomed to use the word fermentation in the other sense, that it would be very difficult to get a more scientifically accurate nomenclature adopted.

Chapter 5

The Causes of Fermentation and Putrefaction

When we leave a body subject to fermentation or putrefaction exposed to the necessary conditions, that is to say, in the presence of warmth and water, we see the appearances of one or the other change after a shorter or longer time, and we can observe that it continues till the body is entirely destroyed.

As the change is begun and completed spontaneously, the cause must be sought for in the substance itself. It was formerly thought that the atoms in the body were in such an unstable state of combination that it was only necessary to set those of a single molecule in motion to ensure the propagation of the movement to the other molecules, until the chemical cohesion of all of them was destroyed. From this point of view the commencement of fermentation or decomposition may be likened to the setting in motion of a whole heap of sand by the sliding at first of a few of the grains on a sloping surface.

Although we are still ignorant of the *modus operandi* in many sorts of fermentation, we know enough to be sure that the above theory is wrong. We at least know the real causes in the case of foods, and are hence in a position to combat them effectually. According to the present universally accepted theory, all fermentation or putrefaction requires the presence of a special substance known as a ferment.

We must divide the ferments into two great groups: the chemical ferments and the organised ferments. The former are definite chemical compounds, which are sometimes already present in decomposing bodies, but only come into operation when the other conditions of moisture and heat are supplied, and sometimes are not formed until then.

These ferments, which we distinguish as organised,–and these are the ones which are of the greatest importance for us,–are living organisms, which must be considered as constituting the lowest type of plants. Our knowledge of these is of very recent date, and we must admit that it is still in its infancy.

Before we pass to the description of the organised ferments, we will briefly consider the chemical ferments.

The Chemical Ferments

In some vegetable substances, and also in some chemical compounds, reactions take place owing to the presence of a certain chemical compound. This appears to have the power of causing change in an unlimited quantity of certain chemical compounds, without itself undergoing any change; it works as a ferment or decomposition producer.

In the sprouting of grain a compound is formed called diastase. This is able to convert starch into sugar and dextrine, a property on which several very important trades, that of the brewer for example, depend.

We know very little of the composition of diastase. It has never been obtained pure, and we only know that it exerts its effect best at temperature in the neighbourhood of 50° C., but that a temperature of 75°, or probably even somewhat less, checks it entirely.

A ferment acting similarly to diastase is a compound called emulsine, found in almonds. This acts on the amygdaline which accompanies it in bitter almonds, and converts it into prussic acid, sugar, and bitter-almond oil.

The formation of mustard oil, which the seeds of the plant do not contain ready made, is also caused by a chemical ferment.

The process of digestion, both in men and in the lower animals, appears to be chiefly due to chemical ferments, the so-called peptones.

We have powerful chemical ferments in the saliva and in the gastric juice.

We may close the description of the chemical ferments by remarking that we have to rely on the future for better information on the nature and action of these compounds.

The Organised Ferments

It has long been known that fermenting and putrefying liquids develop microscopic organisms of very simple structure in enormous numbers. Their presence was, however, considered as accidental, and that they simply settled in such liquids because they found food there. Of late we have learnt by means of highly ingenious experiments that their presence is the cause of the fermentation or putrefaction which always happens whenever they find a suitable resting-place.

We must therefore regard these bodies as ferments, and distinguish them from those first discussed by calling them organised ferments.

The determination of the nature of the organised ferments is in no sense easy, on account of the extreme simplicity of the structure of all of them. They are spherical or oval, rarely cylindrical, bodies with a liquid, interior containing solid particles. Another difficulty lies in their extremely minute size. Most of them require a magnification of 400 or 500 diameters to make them appear even the size of a millet seed. Some are only just visible under the most powerful microscope.

Mould Fungi

These are among the commonest organised ferments. The whitish or greenish flaky covering we see on bread, leather etc., which have been stored in a damp place, consists of various varieties of them. They develop from spores invisible to the naked eye, first to a tissue of delicate threads which appear as white points on the bread or the leather. These points run together, and from the white surface so formed arise, as a sharp eye can clearly discern, fine threads with a spherical knob at the end. These are the spore cases, and are the reproductive part of the plant. The vast number of the spores explains the rapid way in which the mould will occupy large surfaces.

The commonest variety of these fungi is *Penicillium glaucum*. If a spore of this lodges on a favourable situation, it develops first a mass of threads such as is represented in Figure 1. This spawn (*mycelium*) is visible to the naked eye as a very delicate flocculent mass. From it arise upright threads (Figure 2) with arms at the end like the bristles of a brush. These are the spore-carriers (*conidia*), and the spores develop on their ends in the form of greyish-green cells. As a single spore can become a complete plant in forty-eight hours, the rapid growth of the mould on damp bread or cheese is easily understood. Another very common kind is *Mucor mucedo* (Figure 3). Its mycelium spreads like a root with the spore case, which is supported on a stalk and has the form of an orange-yellow knob,

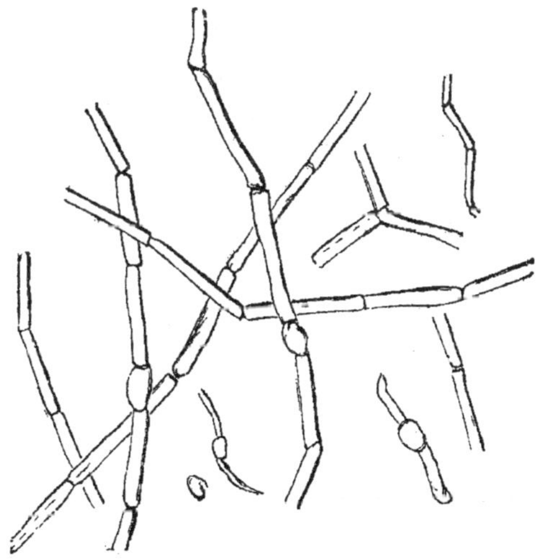

Figure 1

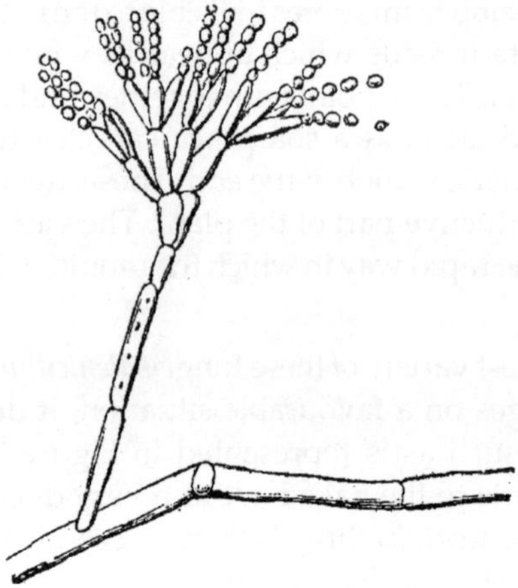

Figure 2

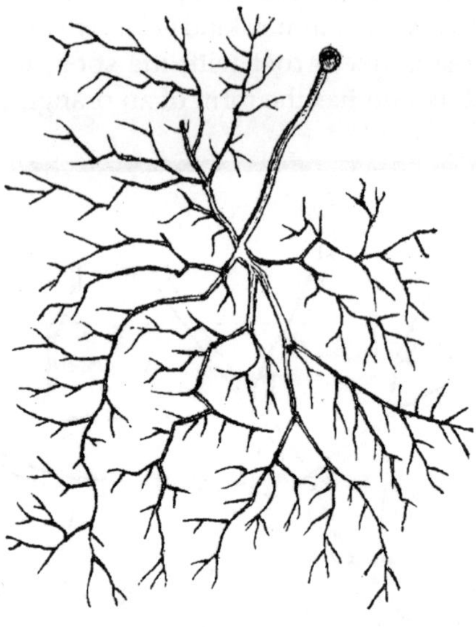

Figure 3

containing numerous spores, which separate from one another when the knob comes into contact with damp, and quickly develop new plants.

The fermentative action of these moulds is a gradual decomposition of the substance on which they flourish into carbonic acid and water without the development of any bad smell. The characteristic mouldy smell which pervades places where these plants are abundant belongs to the plant itself, and is due to one of its own constituents. These fungi have the characteristic property of flourishing in air which is very poor in oxygen, and which would quickly kill more highly organized vegetables. The mould may take the form of fermentation or of putrefaction, according to the body on which the mould is growing, although the term is often used without reference to either putrefaction or fermentation.

SACCHAROMYCES

Ferments in the true sense of the word consist of those organisms which constitute yeast. The latest researches have shown that spirituous fermentation can be brought about by several kinds of fungus. It will be sufficient for our purpose, however, to study the commonest, which is *Saccharomyces cerevisiæ*, represented in Figure 4. It consists of globular or egg-shaped cells, which multiply very rapidly by division. Some of the cells, the so-called mother-cells, emit a process which gradually forms a new cell, and this parts company, assuming an independent existence and the power of giving rise to fresh cells. This ferment in solutions containing the albumenoids and salts which it needs for food, converts sugar into alcohol and carbonic acid. We know, however, that although these two substances are the chief products of the fermentation, certain

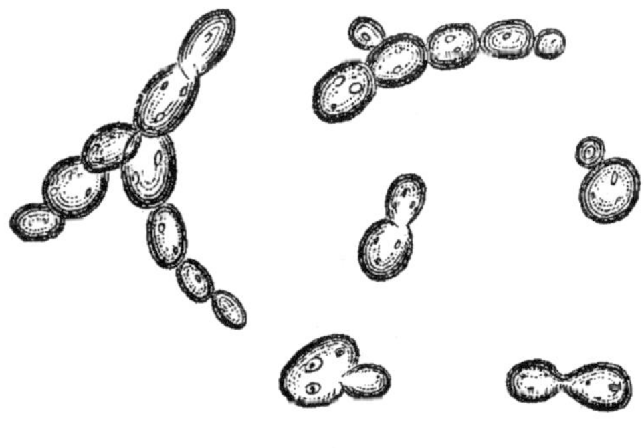

Figure 4

others are invariably formed as well, such as succinic acid and glycerine.

In liquids which have undergone alcoholic fermentation, or which contain acetic acid, we often find another fungus, *Saccharomyces mesambryanthemum,* which in the presence of air converts both alcohol and acetic acid into carbonic acid and water. This ferment, therefore, is one of those concerned in producing the very last stages of decomposition. *S. mesambryanthemum* forms first a thin white scum on the surface of the liquid. This scum gradually thickens and crumples, and often becomes very like the pluck of an animal. The exclusion of air hinders the development of this ferment, as it cannot exist without oxygen.

Schizomycetes

These are simple and extremely small organisms which multiply by each individual dividing into two. Many fermentations are the result of their action, as for example acetic, lactic, and butyric fermentations. They are the cause of all those actions known as putrefaction. They are also most probably the cause of many epidemic diseases, such as cholera, anthrax, plague, etc. We can here only consider those which are of special importance in connection with food-preservation. The acetic ferment (Figure 5) under high magnification appears in the form of little spheres, which form strings like pearls. It inhabits alcoholic liquids, such as beer, wine, and diluted spirits, and in the presence of air converts the alcohol gradually into acetic acid. When immersed in the liquid so as to be

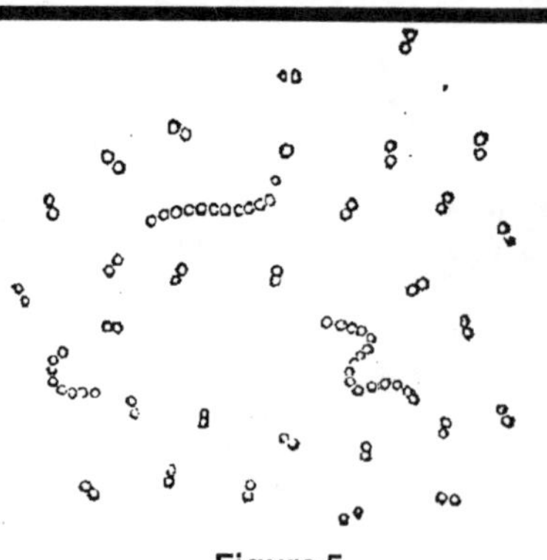

Figure 5

out of contact with the air it forms thick slimy masses, which constitute the so-called vinegar plant.

The mucic ferment develops in sugary liquids, such as imperfectly fermented wine, and in many sweet fruit-juices, and converts them into tough masses which draw out into threads and have much resemblance to molten glue.

The lactic ferment (Figure 6) consists of very minute short rods. It sours milk and vegetables, and helps the acetic ferment to spoil beer.

The butyric ferment (Figure 7) shows under the microscope rather long rods. It is the cause of the spoiling of many foods, and probably also of the rancidity of butter.

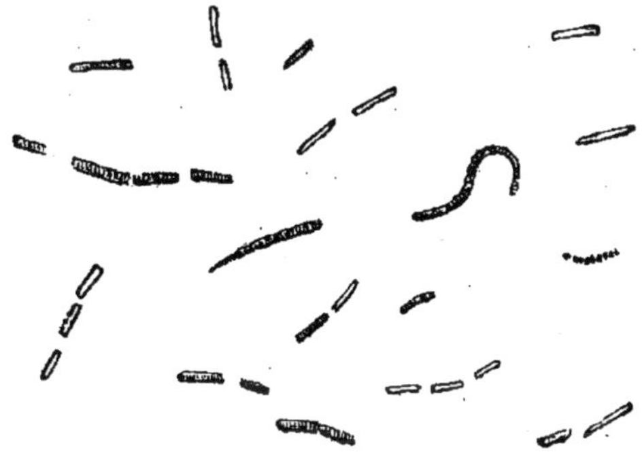

Figure 6

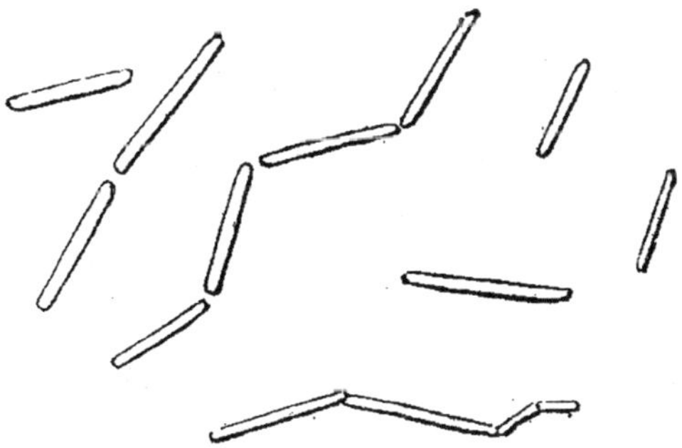

Figure 7

The conditions of the development of these ferments depend upon the nature of the body on which they live, and on the temperature. The fungi of alcoholic fermentation require a sugary liquid; *S. mesambryanthemum* needs liquids containing alcohol or acetic acid; the acetic ferment those containing alcohol, and the lactic ferment those containing sugar, etc. The alcoholic ferments act best between 16° and 20° C., the lactic ferment between 30° and 35°, the acetic ferment between 25° and 30°, and the butyric ferment is about 40°, and when once their development has started it is not stopped even by a considerable fall of temperature, although the action of the ferment becomes much slower. A full halt is, however, not reached until the temperature has fallen to zero.

Putrefaction is a kind of fermentation produced by *schizomycetes,* which are as yet but little known. This is most active at somewhat high temperatures (from 30° to 40° C.). It rapidly falls off as the temperature falls, and entirely ceases at zero. We always find in a putrefying body a number of very different organisms, all of which, however, act as ferments and work either together or in turns on one another's products. An example of this sort of action is seen in the conversion of sugar into alcohol by yeast, next of the alcohol into acetic acid by *Mycoderma aceti,* and, finally, of the acetie acid into carbonic acid and water by *Saccharomyces mesembryanthemum.*

The spores of the ferments float about in the air in untold numbers, and retain their vitality so extraordinarily even when quite dry, that they can avail themselves of favourable opportunities for growth after having been dormant for prolonged periods. Dust which has lain dry for centuries has developed ferments as soon as it was supplied with water. Together with this power of retaining the ability to germinate, these spores have an extraordinarily great resistance to changes of temperature. They stand very intense cold, and will support a temperature of even 50° C. without losing the power of germinating. To germinate they only require water and a temperature a few degrees above the freezing point. If, then, they find these conditions in a body which can also supply them with food, they not only germinate, but multiply with great rapidity, and gradually destroy their host completely. That fermentation and putrefaction are the result of the action of these organisms rests on irresistible experimental evidence, of which we will briefly note the most important points.

If we take bodies such as milk, broth, etc., which rapidly ferment or putrefy when exposed to the air, and heat them to the boiling point of water in a vessel which can be closed air-tight while still hot, the bodies will remain unchanged until air is admitted to them. The high temperature having destroyed all the spores present in the vessel, no change can take place till it is opened to admit more spore-laden air. The same result is produced if we supply the putrefiable substance only with air which has been freed from all living spores. This can be ensured by passing the air through red-hot tubes or through concentrated sulphuric acid. It will be found that the fullest contact with such air will not produce any putrefactive change. The same result can even be brought about by filtering the air through cotton wool.

As we shall see farther on, a large number of the methods of food-preservation depend upon these facts. All that needs to be done is to destroy whatever spores the putrefiable substance already contains and to prevent it from obtaining any more. It can then be kept good for an unlimited period.

There exists, however, a considerable number of bodies which are poisonous to the ferments, and very small amounts of these will often prevent fermentation and thus act as preservative agents. Many, however, of these bodies are poisonous to man also, so that they cannot be used by the preserver of food.

Chapter 6

Preservative Bodies

If we turn first to substances which without absolutely killing the ferments yet hinder their development, we find that all water-absorbing substances are of this nature. Hence a strong solution of sugar or common salt can act as a preservative as efficiently as strong vinegar or any other strong acid. Then, again, many substances can be preserved by simply drying them with sufficient thoroughness.

Those bodies which are actual poisons to ferments often kill them even in very dilute solution. Examples of such bodies are chlorine, sulphurous acid, alum, and most salts of the heavy metals, especially those of copper, zinc, and mercury. Others are boric acid, borax, arsenic, creosote, carbolic acid, salicylic acid, thymol, benzoic acid, and formaldehyde, as well as common salt, sugar, and charcoal. If we bring carbolic acid, for example, to a body in full putrefaction and containing countless organisms, the action abruptly ceases by the killing of the ferments. If a very little carbolic acid is poured into fermenting wort, the production of alcohol at once ceases and the chemical nature of the liquid no longer changes.

As we must admit that putrefaction and fermentation are due in general to the action of ferments, it follows that both those processes are checked by bodies such as we are considering, so that these bodies can be used for disinfection as well as for preservation. Some of them are extensively used as disinfectants, as, for example, chlorine and ferrous sulphate. Chlorine is used at paper mills to disinfect rags, and also by sanitary inspectors in cases of infectious disease.

Ferrous sulphate has a very powerful preventive action against fermentation, and is used in vast quantities for the disinfection of drains and sewers. Our only object in mentioning the subject of disinfection, with which we are not here concerned, is to show the great affinity which exists between fermentation and putrefaction.

The preservative substances already mentioned are not only able to kill organised ferments, but to prevent chemical ferments from acting. Carbolic acid, for example, at once stops the action of diastase, but the rationale of the action is at present quite unknown.

In addition to common salt the bodies most used for food-preservation are sugar, alcohol, vinegar (for pickles), carbolic acid, creosote, and salicylic acid, and we shall devote a few words to each of these chemical preservatives.

Carbolic Acid

Carbolic acid is a product of the dry distillation of coal. Dry distillation means heating with exclusion of air. With coal it gives in the main three products: illuminating gas, tar water, and a thick liquid with a penetrating smell, coaltar. Coal tar is usually black, from the presence of finely divided coal, and contains a great variety of substances, many of which are of the greatest value in the arts. Among them is carbolic acid.

Pure carbolic acid is a pure white crystalline body with a penetrating smell, and is very soluble in water. A concentrated solution of the acid is poisonous to every organism, including man. On account of its poisonous properties it is rarely used in food-preserving, for which purpose it is usually replaced by creosote.

Creosote

Pure creosote is a colourless liquid, which in its chief properties is much like carbolic acid, but consists of a mixture of various dry distillation products, and has a very penetrating smell. It is a very powerful preservative, and can be used in many cases instead of carbolic acid. It occurs in the smoke of a wood fire, especially when beechwood is burned, and in that form is used for curing meat. Strong creosote is a poison, but not quite so powerful a one as carbolic acid.

The preservative action of carbolic acid is very powerful, and is surpassed by no other substance. It appears to be a fact that a liquid containing one-hundredth per cent of carbolic acid is incapable of fermentation, and will keep for a long time even if naturally unusually prone to decomposition. In practice, more carbolic acid however is used than this, or from three to five times as much.

These considerations, and the fact that carbolic acid is the cheapest chemical preservative, would seem to secure its use to the exclusion of all the others. Unfortunately there is a circumstance which restricts its use to a comparatively small number of foods. This difficulty is not its poisonous nature. Poisonousness is only a relative term. Many substances which are extremely active poisons even in small doses, are valuable medicines in still smaller ones, or even inoperative altogether. In the state of dilution in which carbolic acid occurs in preserved food, it is not poisonous. Even prolonged use of such food is unattended with any bad effects. The trouble is the penetrating odour of the acid, which is evident with almost any degree of dilution, and cannot be concealed by other odouriferous bodies. It is well known that a smoked ham will fill a large dining-hall with its pleasant smell, which is solely due to the traces of carbolic acid it contains. This difficulty practically puts carbolic acid out of court for food, except for smoked flesh.

It is of course eminently suitable for objects for which the smoky smell is not objectionable. Wood impregnated with carbolic acid resists the action of damp in an astonishing manner. The use of creosote for food-preservation is, next to salting, the oldest known preserving method. Primitive man soon discovered that meat dried in the smoke of a fire lasted longer than meat dried but not smoked. All smoking processes owe their preservative action to the presence of creosote in the wood smoke.

Salicylic Acid

This substance has long been known, but its preservative power has remained unrecognised until quite lately. It is fitting to discuss it next to carbolic acid, as it is closely related to that substance and approaches it in preserving power. The preparation of salicylic acid used to be a very troublesome process, and was rarely undertaken even in chemical laboratories. It was not until Kolbe discovered its preserving power, and also a process whereby it could be cheaply prepared, that salicylic acid took its place among food-preservatives.

Salicylic acid has now found its way with great rapidity into many branches of art, especially into medicine and perfumery. Pure salicylic acid is a light white, quite odourless solid, having a slightly sweet taste with a somewhat disagreeable after-taste, which is, however, only perceptible with large quantities. Experiment has shown that large quantities of the acid can be taken daily both by men and animals without any bad effects becoming perceptible.[1]

The solubility of salicylic acid in water is very small. Water only dissolves about one-third of a per cent of its own weight at ordinary temperatures. In strong alcohol, however, the acid dissolves freely, and it is fairly soluble in oils and glycerine. Nevertheless, the solubility in water is quite sufficient for preserving purposes. Although salicylic acid is inferior to carbolic acid in preserving power, it is second to nothing else.

Its great advantage as a preservative is its odourlessness. It can be used for the preservation of any kind of food whatever, and it would seem that its introduction will revolutionise the food-preserving industry, as all that is necessary is to add salicylic acid to the food in a proper manner. It is thus obvious that salicylic acid deserves the greatest attention on the part of food-preservers. Many experiments have shown that the acid has all the power that has been claimed for it. The price is about 4s. per lb., which, when we compare it with the value of the food which a pound will preserve, is absolutely insignificant.

Although, as above stated, salicylic acid has no injurious action on the organism, its use for preserving food has been for the last few years forbidden by law in very many countries. Hence food which is intended for sale should not be preserved with salicylic acid.

Sulphurous Acid

This is a gas produced by burning sulphur, and has a characteristic suffocating smell. It dissolves readily in water, and still more freely in spirit, and is occasionally used to preserve certain

[1] This has recently been denied by many competent authorities.–Tr.

things, grape juice and hops for example, by exposing them to the fumes of burning brimstone.

Sulphurous acid acts very energetically and poisonously upon ferments. A very little of it will at once arrest fermentation or putrefaction by killing the organisms concerned. Simple as the method of using the gas for preservation is, its use is only limited and will never become more general. The causes are the smell of the gas, although it is less intense than that of carbolic acid, and also the fact that sulphurous acid is itself a very unstable substance.

As foods which have to be preserved always contain water, sulphurous acid can only exist in them as the hydrate (H_2SO_3). Now this absorbs oxygen from the air and becomes sulphuric acid (H_2SO_4), which has no preservative action. We thus see why grape juice which has been sulphured ultimately ferments. Both the cellarman and the hop merchant make use of sulphurous acid, but its instability unfits it for general use. In fact, it finds large employment only as a bleaching agent.

Benzoic Acid and Thymol

These are two substances which have been proposed by Fleck for food-preservation, but are as yet too expensive for adoption. There is also another objection to thymol, namely, that it has a characteristic, if not altogether unpleasant, smell, which would infallibly make itself perceptible in food preserved by means of thymol. Benzoic acid has long been used as a preservative by perfumers, to prevent pomades from becoming rancid.

Boric Acid

This is a mineral acid, taking, when pure, the form of white mother-of-pearl-like flakes, which are not very soluble in water, have a barely perceptible sour taste, and have no injurious action on the human organism. Many minerals contain salts of boric acid, and the acid itself occurs in the hot vapours issuing from the ground in certain volcanic districts. In Tuscany these vapours are passed into water, which, when subsequently evaporated, gives crude boric acid, which is then purified by recrystallisation. Boric acid has of late assumed great importance as a preserving agent, not only for food, but for substances used in the arts. It is employed either in the solid form, powdered, or in solution in water or spirit.

Borax

This is sodium biborate, and is a white crystalline solid, soluble in water. It resembles free boric acid in its preserving power, and is used in the same way. The expensive proprietary solutions puffed as preserving-liquids for meat, milk, etc., nearly all contain common salt, together with borax or boric acid.

Fluorine Compounds

Hydrofluoric acid and other fluorides are very powerful preservatives, and deserve notice for preserving anatomical and zoological specimens, and also hides.

Formaldehyde

This substance, also known as formaline, comes on the market in the form of a colourless liquid consisting of 60 per cent of water and 40 per cent of formaldehyde, and having a very characteristic odour. The preserving power is so great that a very efficient fluid is made by diluting commercial formaline with four hundred times its weight of water. As, however, formaldehyde is a poison, it cannot be used for food-preservation. It finds the same uses as the fluorine compounds.

Metallic Salts

Whether metallic salts should be used or not for food-preservation is a question which is answered by the fact that nearly all of them are poisonous, and have, moreover, a very disagreeable taste. For these reasons they are useless for our purpose, but they often render excellent service in the preservation of hides and wood. They are used for railway sleepers and many other purposes. As they cannot be used for food-preservation, we have only two more important preservatives to describe: sugar and salt.

Sugar

The name sugar is applied to a whole series of chemical compounds, occurring both in the animal and the vegetable kingdoms. They behave in an almost similar manner towards other bodies, but can be distinguished from one another by distinct chemical reactions. Even the sweet taste which belongs to all sugars, exists in very different degrees. Fruit-sugar, for example, has a very strong sweet taste, while the sweetness of milk-sugar is very slight. All sugars in dilute solution undergo fermentation very readily, and the products depend on what the sugar is, the nature of the ferment, and the temperature. Some of them are: alcohol, glycerine, lactic acid, acetic acid, and butyric acid. Concentrated solutions of sugar are prejudicial to fermentation, and hence are preservatives in the true sense of the word. This difference between dilute and concentrated solutions is to be ascribed to the fact that the latter have a great affinity for water, which they subtract from the bodies of any ferments that may find access to them, thereby either killing them or rendering them inactive. This property of concentrated solution of sugar is most extensively made use of in preserving fruit and fruit-juices, in candying fruit, and for many other purposes. When we speak of sugar without qualification, we mean here the sugar used for sweetening dishes, *i.e.*, saccharose, cane or beet sugar. Fruits and honey contain a different kind, namely, grape-sugar or glucose, which has the sweetest taste of all the sugars. Milk contains the slightly sweet and difficultly soluble milk-sugar.

Salt

Salt occurs in commerce either as sea-salt or rock-salt. It is a compound of sodium and chlorine. It is fairly soluble in water, and strong solutions of it have a great affinity for water, so that the preserving action of brine has the same cause as that of sugar, and whether sugar or salt is used for preserving depends upon the taste we desire in the food after treatment. The combination of the taste of sugar with that of most fruits is agreeable to our palates, as is that of the taste of salt and the taste of meat. Hence, as a general rule, we use sugar to preserve fruit and salt to preserve meat, although we could preserve fruit in salt or meat in sugar perfectly well. For preserving some fruits indeed, cucumbers for example, salt is actually used.

Alcohol

Alcohol is another substance with very efficient preservative action. No ferment can live in a liquid containing 25 per cent of alcohol, and alcohol is hence an excellent preservative for many things, such as fruit. A very large number of substances act like alcohol, but few of these can be used as preservatives, strong acetic acid for example, as the others are all poisonous to the organism.

Like concentrated solutions of salt or sugar, there are other bodies which act preservatively by abstracting water. To one of these we may now specially allude.

Glycerine

Glycerine is a constituent of fats, and is a by-product of the manufacture of stearine candles. In the pure state, in which it can now be cheaply bought, it is a colourless syrupy liquid of a very sweet burning taste. It absorbs water greedily, with evolution of heat. It is without action on the organism.

That glycerine acts against fermentation, like brine or concentrated sugar solution, is obvious, but unlike salt or sugar it acts even in dilute solution, so that fruit and meat can be preserved in water containing only a relatively small quantity of glycerine.

Wood-Charcoal

This, thanks to two of its properties, is used as a preservative in the form of powder. The method of its preparation causes it to contain creosote if in traces only. This gives it a certain preservative action. Moreover, like all very porous and finely divided substances, wood charcoal absorbs large quantities of oxygen.

If, therefore, we surround some readily putrefiable substance, such as fresh meat, with powdered wood charcoal, the trace of creosote therein will do its work, and those ferment spores which escape its action will be unable to develop for want of oxygen, which will all be absorbed by the wood charcoal.

We close with this short description of wood-charcoal, the list of the bodies which are used in practice as preservatives. We trust and hope that the progress of chemistry will supply us with others which will be better for our purpose than any we yet know. Salicylic acid is an earnest of what we may expect.

If once we succeed in discovering a preservative which will answer for all kinds of food, the discovery will be of a value which it is impossible to overrate. We shall then be able to transport the fruits of the trees of the tropics and fresh meat from South America or Australia to any part of the world we may desire, and to avoid in the simplest possible manner the constant heavy losses involved in the putrefaction of food. Hitherto we know of no preservative which can be used for any food under all circumstances, and the only approach we have to such a substance is salicylic acid.

Chapter 7

The Various Methods of Preserving Food

As might have been expected from the diversity of food-preservatives, there are numerous processes for preserving food, either with the help of these preservatives or by simply adopting certain mechanical methods. These methods are in many cases far better than the employment of chemical preservatives, and they would probably be exclusively adopted if they did not bring about undesired changes in some foods, and if they did not in most cases involve the use of rather expensive plant.

If we leave for the present those processes which consist in adding preservative substances, and consider those in which the preserving is effected without the addition of any other substance, we see that the latter can be classified under three heads:

1. Preservation by heat or cold.
2. Preservation by drying.
3. Preservation by excluding air.

Each of these methods has its advantages and its disadvantages, and the selection must depend upon the nature of the food to be preserved.

The Preservation of Food by Deprivation of Heat

It is a well-known fact that every chemical process and every decomposition of a food is retarded by lowering the temperature. It is the reason for storing food in places as cold as possible. The ferment spores, which cause nearly all the spoiling of food, enter into a dormant state at temperatures approaching the freezing point of water, *i.e.* they cease to grow, without, however, losing their power to resume doing so. Hence even readily putrefiable substances can be kept for a very long time, even for months, at such temperatures in a perfectly fresh state. In many cases we can bring the temperature so low as to freeze the juices contained in the food, which will then keep for practically an unlimited time. As an example of this we may quote the fact that the corpse of a mammoth was found frozen in ice in Siberia, and the flesh was still quite fresh. When we reflect that the mammoth is an animal which has not existed on the earth since an unthinkable time ago, we must admit that this corpse had remained in the ice for many thousands of years without decomposing.

In Northern lands people keep fish, flesh, and fowl in a frozen state unchanged throughout the whole of winter, and can send them long distances in this condition. Frozen fish arrive in St. Petersburg all through the winter from the Caspian and Black Seas.

Some foods, however, cannot be preserved advantageously by mere freezing. They must be kept very near that point, but if they actually freeze their taste becomes changed. Food-stuffs which will not bear a temperature below zero (C.) are generally stored in cellars. Those which will may, if the climate admit, be frozen by simply exposing them to the natural cold in the winter.

Experience has shown that food which has been preserved by freezing, must be soon consumed when once it has been thawed, as it goes bad much more quickly in this case than the same article in a fresh state. We think that the reason of this is that the expansion of the liquids on freezing bursts the cell walls and the vessels, so that the ferments come into full contact with every part of the food much more rapidly. Under ordinary circumstances the ferments take a long time to penetrate the mass completely, but this penetration is obviously greatly facilitated by the wholesale breaking down of structure induced by freezing.

The deprivation of heat is brought about in very different ways. One of the simplest plans is to store the food in very deep cellars possessing a low uniform temperature. By providing such cellars with suitable ventilators, they can be made very cold in the winter, and will keep a low temperature throughout the summer.

The use of ice is deservedly extending, and of late we have learned several very ingenious ways of using it for the preservation of food. To this subject we shall return later.

Preservation of Food by Momentary Heating

Food can be preserved by a process the exact opposite of that just described, namely, by heating it to a temperature previously decided on. While in preservation at low temperatures the ferments are simply hindered in development, they are killed by this process. If the food is then stored in a suitable manner, it will be preserved. Of course this process is useless if fresh supplies of spores are allowed to replace those which have been killed. The food must be stored in such a way that ferments cannot obtain access to it.

This is a very commonly used method of food-preservation, as it is suitable for a very large number of comestibles.

Preservation by the Subtraction of Water

We have already mentioned that certain substances, sugar and salt for example, preserve food by their concentrated solutions absorbing and retaining water, and thus depriving the ferments of that substance so necessary for their existence. This kind of preservation can be effected without these bodies by the aid of heat. The desiccation of foods by artificial heat is one of the simplest methods known, and is therefore extensively employed. Under suitable conditions the drying may be done in the open air by natural heat. In most cases it is quite unnecessary to evaporate the whole of the water present. It is sufficient that the substances, which in the undried food are in weak solution, should assume the form of solutions sufficiently concentrated to resist fermentation action. By this method we preserve meat, fish, fruit, vegetables, fruit-juices, and various vegetable extracts, and in this way we can preserve perfectly even the most putrefiable bodies, the albumens for example.

Preserving Food by the Exclusion of Air

All ferments probably require contact with free oxygen in order to develop, although many of them want very little, and that only in the earlier stages of their growth. Hence if we keep food absolutely guarded from all access of air, it will not go bad. In many cases this method is combined with the heating method just noticed, *i.e.*, the ferments present are killed by heat, and then the exclusion of the air prevents the arrival of any more.

Preservative Liquids

Solid foods can also be preserved by pickling them in suitable liquids. As we shall have to return to this part of our subject, we shall here treat it very briefly.

For meat, fish, cucumbers, and plums we use concentrated brine, and concentrated syrup for all sorts of sweet fruits, and also vinegar, to every litre of which some salt and two or three gram of salicylic acid should be added, for all kinds of meat, and also for plums and cucumbers, and alcoholic liquids for sweet fruits etc. The ready-made liquids sold at high prices, such as the once famous Wickersheimer solution, usually contain salicylic acid, and many of them boric acid or borax as well. We deprecate the use of such liquids most decidedly, because they entail risk of trouble with the sanitary authorities. Only substances should be used of which the composition is known, and which can be guaranteed to contain no illicit substance.

We have now briefly indicated the various means available for food-preservation, and we have found that there are five principal methods as follow:

1. The use of some antiseptic, such as carbolic acid, salicylic acid, creosote, etc.
2. The abstraction of heat, storage in cold cellars, ice-houses, freezing chambers, etc.
3. Heating to a temperature high enough to kill all ferments.
4. Exclusion of air; a process usually combined with the last.
5. Pickling in suitable liquids.

It has appeared to us of great importance to look upon these various methods at first from a general point of view, so that in the remainder of the book we may be able to confine ourselves to practical details, describing the special methods to be followed in any given case. We shall in part consider vegetable-preservation apart from that of animal food, as this plan is fully justified by the sharp differences in chemical composition existing between vegetable and animal matter.

Chapter 8

The Preservation of Animal Food

Animal foods are of great importance, as they form the largest part of our nourishment. They are also specially liable to rapid decomposition, and thus stand in need of the preserver's art. The chief sorts of animal food are meat, milk, eggs, cheese, and fat.

These products, the highest efforts of the organising powers of nature, consist of an immense number of very different bodies, many of which have hardly any property in common but that of being easily putrescible. In the most important of them all–meat–we find a large number of albuminous bodies, and a number of others, such as creatine, creatinine, sarkine, lactic acid, and salt.

With the exception of salt, all these are highly putrefiable, as is also the fat, from which no meat is entirely free. The large amount of water in fresh meat helps the decomposition greatly, and consequently it often goes bad in warm weather in a few hours.

Flesh is a far more important article of food than the other food-stuffs got from animals, and we shall therefore begin with the methods for preserving meat. The question of meat-preservation has of late become one of literally vital moment to Europe, and may have the same importance at no very distant period in the United States. There the population is increasing at such a rate that the production of fresh meat in the country itself will soon probably become insufficient for it.

How important meat-preservation is in the provisioning of ships which have to make long voyages, needs no more mention than it does in connection with large armies in the field, the supply of fortified places, or of large towns in general.

At present we cannot look upon the problem of meat-preservation as more than half solved. It is true that we are in a position to preserve meat for long periods after cooking it, but we cannot keep raw meat for long periods. When we can store raw meat without change for at least several months, we may look upon the remaining half of the problem as sufficiently solved for all practical purposes.

When we have achieved this final success,–and that we shall ultimately do so is beyond all doubt,–it will be possible to sell meat everywhere so cheaply that it will no longer be possible to say that thousands of people never eat meat except on festival days, for everybody will get it every day.

Next to meat and fish in order of importance among animal foods come milk, eggs, and butter.

Every conceivable process has been tried for the preservation of meat, and a study of the methods attempted gives a clear insight into the present position of the preserving art. No further proof is wanted that other bodies nearly as prone to putrefaction as meat can be preserved in the same way as meat, and that it is only necessary to have regard to the special properties of the food in hand in order to decide what method to adopt.

Hence when we, in the following pages, speak of meat only, we are taking it as a type, and our remarks would often apply equally to milk, eggs, fruits, vegetables, and other foods which very readily decompose, and hence require great care both in storing and in preserving.

Chapter 9

Preserving Meat by Means of Ice

A low temperature is a very simple and sure means of preserving food for a long time. The Greenlanders consider it a special advantage of their country, and one to be proud of, that even there meat will go bad, although it freezes every night, even in the height of summer.

In Europe, where we have during most of the year a temperature which is no hindrance to putrefaction, we are compelled to obtain low temperatures for food-preservation by artificial means, none of which are cheaper than the use of ice.

We cannot refrain here from some remarks on this subject, as we are of opinion that ice can be used with great advantage. In our journeys over Europe, we have had many opportunities of observing that ice might find much more employment not merely as a luxury, but for material well-being.

It is remarkable that Germany, where the climate readily permits the storage of ice on a large scale, uses little in comparison with countries which have to import all the ice they need. In this respect many nations can teach us a useful lesson. In Denmark, for example, we have seen huge dishes of ice placed on the tables of the inns in summer, simply for the purpose of cooling the air.

England, which is prevented by its maritime climate from producing much ice, in spite of its northerly position, imports that article from Norway and North America. In this trade a large number of ships is exclusively engaged. In Italy, again, every common inn uses plenty of the purest clear ice for cooling beverages. In Sicily ice is harvested from the narrow glacier belt of Etna, and is also imported. In India ice is either brought from the Himalayas or made in ice machines. In these hot countries ice is a necessary of daily life and not a luxury.

In Germany, where nearly every winter offers a large harvest of ice, we should think it a great luxury if we all could cool our summer drinks with ice. In Naples and Palermo, however, every street seller throughout the summer provides his customers with iced beverages at a minimum charge. Ice is a substance which can contribute notably to the enjoyment of life, and merits a far more extended use than for keeping meat for a few days, or for making freezing mixtures for confectioners.

Ice-Cellars

Many difficulties are experienced in keeping ice through the winter when the usual irrational methods are adopted. We propose, therefore, to say a few words about storage.

If ice has to be stored near the place of production, the filling of the store should not be begun until the weather is, from previous years' experience, probably at its coldest. If the ice is just at the freezing point when stored, the least rise of temperature will thaw part of it. If, on the other hand, it is stored on a very cold winter's day, say at 10° below 0°C., the case is very different. This very cold ice, too, has the advantage that it is closer and more solid than ice at the freezing point.

To heat ice from 10° below 0 to that point it must come into contact with ten times as much air as is required to produce the first drops of water from ice already at zero, the air being at the same temperature in either case. Hence we find that ice stacked at very low temperatures keeps perfectly dry for months, while under the same circumstances ice stored at zero has thawed to a large extent.

Heat reaching the first lot of ice, has to raise it to zero before fusion commences, but that process begins at once when the ice was at zero when stored.

In most places it is usual to break up the large slabs of ice gathered from frozen-water surfaces, and to fill the storeroom with the fragments. But every scientist knows that the susceptibility of a body to external influences increases with the surface which it offers. This fact is borne in mind when solids are powdered as a preliminary to dissolving them. This treatment of ice, then, facilitates its fusion, and it should always be stored in the largest possible pieces. These should be stacked as closely as possible, and all the interstices filled up with smaller pieces or snow.

Ice is generally stored in cellars. As these only rise slightly above the mean temperature of the year in the summer, they answer well enough if the cellar is managed properly, which, however, is not often the case. It often happens that the ice is so stowed that it comes into contact with the walls. These, however, are fairly food conductors of heat from without, and the consequence is that the ice thaws all round the walls. The proper plan is to erect a wooden partition about two inches thick, running parallel to the walls, at a distance of about a foot from them. When the ice is stored inside the wood, it is protected from the warmth of the walls by a layer of air, which is an extremely bad conductor. The ice then keeps infinitely better than when it touches the walls.

Other difficulties may, however, be met with in a cellar. If the floor is very porous, *e.g.*, of a sandy or gravelly soil, all water resulting from the fusion of any of the ice at once escapes. This water, which is at zero, is wasted so far as its effect in keeping the cellar cold is concerned.

If the floor of the cellar is impervious to water,–which is the case when it consists of clay,–the water does not escape, but another nuisance is caused, as it has to be pumped up when it has accumulated in large quantities. If the soil is full of springs, or surface water rises through it, the making of an ice-cellar in it is almost a matter of impossibility, for it is a very expensive matter to build a cellar with water-tight walls and floor. Such expenditure has not been shirked sometimes in large breweries, but it is entirely unnecessary.

The practical Americans, who know better than we do how to apply natural laws to commercial uses, have discovered the best of all ways of storing ice, whereby it can be kept from one winter to another with a minimum of waste. They do not use cellars; but ice-houses, which are so constructed that their interiors are shielded from external changes of temperature. Many people fancy that the construction of these houses is a secret. This, however, is not the case, and we proceed to give an illustrated description of the American system.

Ice-Houses

In building a storage place for ice which is above the surface, the whole interior must, as far as possible, be surrounded by bad conductors of heat. Hence there is no better material for them than wood, two or three inches of which excludes heat as completely as a wall of ten times the thickness.

To prevent heat passing from the soil to the interior of the ice-house,–which may happen even in the winter,–the floor must have a clear space of about a yard between it and the ground. The warmth of the atmosphere is excluded by making the walls double, with an air space in between. Even greater security may be obtained by packing the space between the walls with waste tan, sawdust, or dry turf. The ice-house has a wooden ceiling well below the roof, which has a very thick thatch. To keep off the rays of the sun, the ice-house should be planted round with trees that form a thick and close canopy, such as horse-chestnuts. The entrance to the ice-house is through double doors separated by a passage several yards long. The inside of each door is covered with a thick matting of straw. From the inner ceiling of the house a chimney of boards, about sixteen inches square, reaches above the roof, and is provided with a closely fitting damper.

Figure 8 shows in section such an ice-house as we have described. *A* is the outer wall of strong beams, and *J* is the thinner wooden inner wall, which is two inches or three inches thick, and at least a yard from the outer wall. The outer wall is caulked with moss and painted white. *G* represents the passage of entrance, and *T T* the two doors; *S* is the chimney, closed by damper *K*.

Even in places which have as warm a climate as Naples, ice can be kept in such a house for at least a year, without losing more

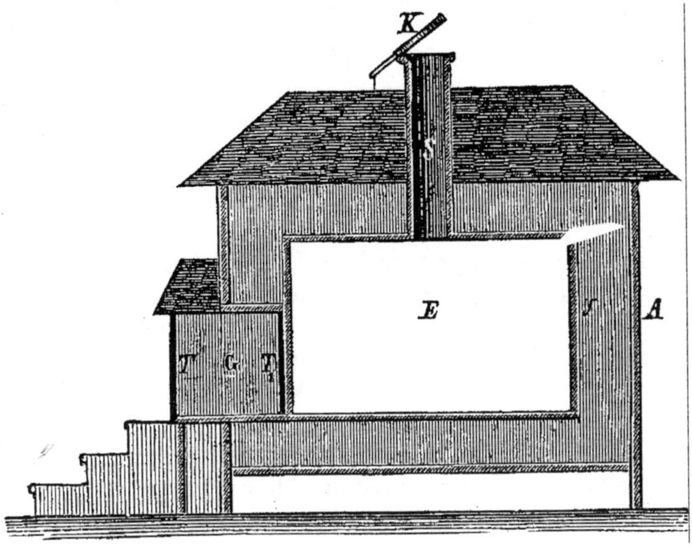

Figure 8

than half of it. To utilise the cold of the water formed by the fusion of the ice, it is desirable that perforations in the floor should allow it to gain access to the packing of the double walls. It then rises in the packing by capillary attraction, and gradually evaporates through holes provided for that purpose in the outer walls. These holes are about an inch in diameter, and at a distance of seven to eight feet from the floor. They are spaced from twenty to thirty inches apart.

If we store any food in an ice-house, it very soon becomes cooled to the freezing point of water, and the development of fermentation is arrested. If it is completely surrounded by the ice it may be kept fresh for weeks, even if of a very putrefiable nature. Care must be taken that it cannot come into contact with any ice-water.

It is, however, impossible by simply keeping meat in rooms, the temperature of which is zero (C.), to retain its freshness for an indefinite time. In a few weeks the smell of putrefaction becomes evident, and the meat finally putrifies entirely, although of course much more slowly than would be the case at a higher temperature. Many attempts have been made to send fresh meat from South America to Europe, by constructing places on shipboard on the principles of the ice-house and hanging the freshly killed carcasses therein. These attempts ended in complete failure. The next idea was to put the meat, not into the ice-house itself, but in a separate chamber, and to maintain a constant current of air, cooled to zero in the ice-house, through the storage chamber by means of pumps. This plan has succeeded rough better, it appears, and London receives large supplies of meat from America and Australia preserved in this way.

It is certain that the preservation of meat in a fresh state for long periods requires its maintenance at a temperature of at least –2°C. Improvements in refrigerating machinery have made it possible to secure this result. On ships trading between Australia and England, a system of tubes is provided which is kept at a temperature of –10° C. or lower, by the circulation of a solution of calcium chloride. These tubes being in the storage chamber soon make the air cold enough to freeze the carcasses hung up within. All that has to be done is to keep the refrigerating machinery in constant action through the voyage.

In sending natural ice great distances by rail or sea, the best way to preserve it is to have it in as large blocks as possible, and to pack them in sawdust. We have seen large blocks of ice unshipped in London in the middle of summer, which had suffered hardly any waste.

In preserving meat by means of ice it is essential, as above stated, to keep it from all contact with ice-water. The best plan is to have a refrigerator, *i.e.*, a double box. The meat is placed in the inner box and the space between this and the outer box is filled with ice. Small animals and birds or fish can be wrapped in vegetable parchment and laid directly upon the ice.

Refrigerators

To keep large masses of fresh meat for a few days, in the markets of large towns for example, refrigerators are used, which are kept at or below zero by means of suitable machinery. The same result may be obtained in a cellar over which ice is stored. In Figure 9, *K* represents a cellar over which an ice-house is built, the floor of which is supported on T-irons having interspaces of from four to six inches. Under them gutters are placed to catch the ice-water from the house and carry it off. The air cooled by the ice sinks into the cellar and keeps the air in it at zero. Household refrigerators or ice cupboards

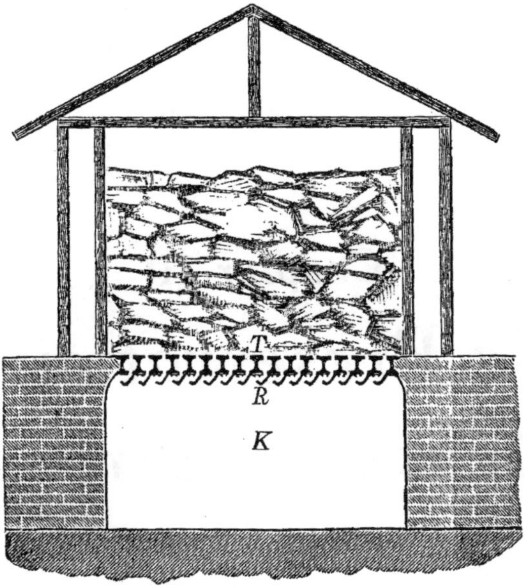

Figure 9

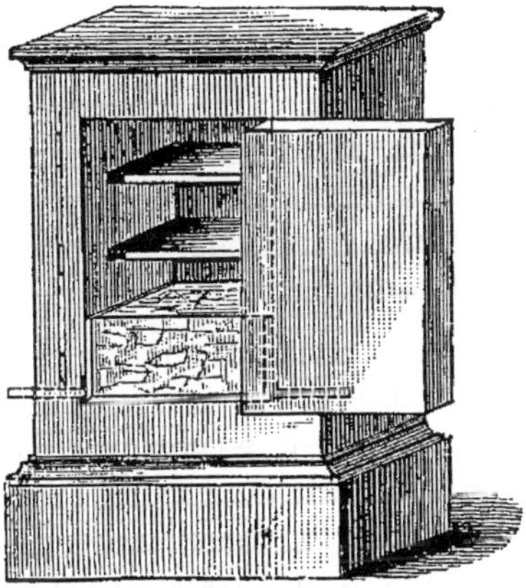

Figure 10

are merely ice-houses on a smaller scale. The double walls are separated by a packing of some badly conducting material. Figure 10 shows such a cupboard. The apparatus acts more efficiently, however, when the ice is above the articles to be cooled.

Chapter 10

The Preservation of Meat by Charcoal

Wood-charcoal has an extraordinarily great power of absorption, not merely for gases, but also for scents and dyes. If bad-smelling meat is buried in charcoal powder, the smell soon disappears. Dirty water filtered through charcoal becomes drinkable, and red wine filtered through it becomes colourless.

The anti-putrefactive action of charcoal is partly due to this absorptive action. If a putrescible body is surrounded with charcoal, the latter prevents all access of oxygen, and the ferments cannot develop. Part of the action, however, seems to us to depend on the presence of traces of volatile empyreumatic bodies which are formed when the charcoal is made, the process being a kind of dry distillation. These bodies are rich in creosote, which is a preservative for food. Attempts have been made to utilise the preserving power of charcoal by filling a large case lined with sheet iron with alternating layers of fresh meat and charcoal, taking care that both the lowest and the uppermost layer are of charcoal. The case is finally soldered down.

The results obtained vary much. In some cases the meat has kept fresh for months, even through long sea voyages in the tropics. In others the meat was uneatable in a week or two. This uncertainty hardly permits of the method being recommended for long periods, but it answers excellently for short periods, *e.g.*, when it is necessary to send meat on an ordinary journey by rail.

In using the meat all that has to be done is to wash the charcoal dust from it. The meat must then, however, be cooked at once, or it will soon go bad, especially in summer.

The methods already described have the advantage of keeping the meat in a completely unchanged state, so that it can be cooked without further trouble. They demand, however, a certain amount of skill in the preserver, a quality which is rarest in the countries possessing the largest quantities of meat. In such countries we find very different processes in use, which, although they do not preserve the meat unchanged, keep it in a comparatively raw state. These methods are common both to American and Asiatic nations, and consist in abstracting sufficient water from the meat to keep it from decomposition.

Chapter 11
Preservation of Meat by Drying

The Europeans who emigrated to America learnt from the Indians a method of preserving flesh which is still carried out today in almost its original form. It consists in cutting the meat into long thin strips, which are then dried in the sun or over a fire. It is then called pemmican in the States and tassajo in Spanish America, and forms the staple food in journeys through uncultivated country.

On the cod-fishing coasts near Newfoundland, fish is preserved in the same way. The fish is split into halves, and dried to a hard mass, which resists putrefaction as long as it is kept dry. The taste of pemmican is not agreeable to Europeans, and we doubt whether even the poorest people here would adopt it as a food. It is, however, possible so to modify the original process that the meat will retain its original taste almost completely, and an excellent food can thereby be made which is very suitable for provisioning ships and armies in the field.

Hassal's Patent Process for Preparing Powdered Meat

This process yields a kind of pemmican which has a very excellent taste. As in all cases of preserving meat by drying, care must be taken that the meat is as free as possible from fat veins and sinews. Fat especially is very prone to decomposition. The meat is then cut up in a mincing machine to a paste, which is dried in a drying-room in thin layers spread on tinned iron. A very convenient method is to drive hot air over the layers by means of a fan. The only precaution necessary is that the temperature must never exceed 60°C. at the most, as anything above that coagulates the albuminous constituents of the meat and makes them insoluble, as when white of egg is boiled. The drying is prolonged at between 50° and 60° until the meat shrinks greatly in volume and becomes a crusty mass, which is then ground to powder in a mill, dried again, and filled into the metal cases or paper cylinders lined with tinfoil. If this meat-powder is simmered for a long time in water between 50° and 60° C., it forms a meat soup of unsurpassable quality.

Although this powdered meat will keep a very long time perfectly dry, a still more durable preparation is obtained by heating about a third of the meat used to 70°–75° to coagulate its albumen, and then treating it with the rest as above described. The taste and aroma after preparation leave nothing to be desired.

Verdeil's Process

This differs little from the preceding. The meat is cut into slices across the direction of the muscular fibres, and the slices are cooked in steam of from three to four atmospheres' pressure for about a quarter of an hour. The flesh thus loses most of its water, and remains in a contracted state with a colour approaching grey. It is finally dried completely with hot air, and pressed with the admixture of a little salt into iron canisters.

Chapter 12

The Preservation of Meat by the Exclusion of Air

The presence of air is necessary for fermentation. From a knowledge of this fact a whole series of preserving processes based on the idea of investing meat with an air-tight covering has been devised. Simple as this looks at first sight, the nature of meat opposes many obstacles to its realisation. We know very few bodies which we can use to cover meat for long periods with an air-tight casing. Among them are glue, gelatine, white of egg, indiarubber, pyroxyline, and paraffin. To preserve meat with glue or gelatine, large pieces are chosen free from fat, and dipped in the solution, having a temperature of from 60° to 65°, and strong enough to leave a leathery coating on the meat. After an immersion of a few seconds the meat is lifted out and exposed to a stream of cold air, so that the gelatine may set as quickly as possible. If the meat is not completely covered, it is dipped again. When the coating is quite dry, the meat is packed in sawdust.

The Robert Process

This consists in first killing all ferments already in the meat with the fumes of burning sulphur, and then covering it with an air-tight varnish. The meat is hung up in a room into which the sulphurous acid is led from an opening in the floor, till it can be detected by the sense of smell as it issues from the chimney. The action of the sulphurous acid on the meat lasts about a quarter of an hour. The meat is then hung up in the air till it almost ceases to smell of the gas, and then varnished with a solution of dried albumen and sugar in decoction of marsh-mallow root. It would be much better to drive fresh air through the same room in which the sulphuring is done for some time after the sulphur dioxide has been cut off, and to varnish the meat by dipping it into a pure solution of albumen. In varnishing with the brush there is danger of leaving out parts of the surface which can then bring about the destruction of the whole mass.

A variation of this process consists in dipping the meat first into boiling water, to coagulate its albuminoids at the exterior of the mass, thus providing a protective varnish, and then exposing for some time to the action of sulphurous acid.

The Redwood Process

This consists in preserving meat with a coating of paraffin. The meat is freed from fat and hung in fused paraffin at a temperature of from 130° to 140° C., as long as a characteristic crackling sound shows that steam is escaping from the meat. The meat is then removed, and when quite cold, dipped again, but this time into paraffin which is only just fused. The coating thus obtained is elastic, and adheres very firmly. When the meat is to be used, it is dipped into water hot enough to fuse off the paraffin. As it is already partly cooked by the heat of the first paraffin bath, it wants very little further treatment to prepare it for the table. This is a process which cannot be too highly recommended, both on account of its cheapness, the ease with which it is operated, and the excellence of the results.

Besides the methods already described, and which are in practical use on a large scale, many others have been proposed, such as dipping meat in collodion or in a solution of indiarubber in carbon bisulphide, when a skin of pyroxyline or indiarubber remains on the meat after the solvent has evaporated. This skin is, however, very thin, and would easily get broken.

It has been proposed to treat the meat first with solutions of antiseptics, and then to varnish it. The antiseptics suggested have been solutions of alum or sulphate of alumina. The meat is to be dipped repeatedly in the antiseptic, and finally coated over with glue.

Salts of alumina have all an unpleasant sweetish taste, which is communicated to the meat. Common salt in the form of brine is just as effective.

An excellent method for preserving small quantities of meat is immersion in fused fat, which, when cold, invests the flesh with an air-tight covering. *Pâtes de foie gras* are made on this principle by pouring hot grease over roast goose liver and minced truffles.

Of all these methods depending on the exclusion of air, the Redwood process seems to us the most suitable for use on a large scale, on account of its cheapness.

Chapter 13

The Appert Method

Of all methods for preserving meat the one which gives the most unfailing success is Appert's. We know from experience that every kind of food can be preserved by it, probably for an unlimited time. Like every other method, Appert's process has its shortcomings. It requires an absolutely air-tight case of considerable strength, the provision of which is a notable expense. Nevertheless, the system is invaluable for long voyages, and its discoverer has every right to be called a benefactor of his kind. Scurvy has almost disappeared even on the longest voyages, since food preserved by his process has been used on board ship. The method consists in soldering up the food in tinned iron cans with great care, and then heating the cans for a considerable time in boiling water. Any kind of food can be treated in this way. The duration of the heating depends on the size of the can, for every part of its contents must be kept at the temperature of boiling water for a sufficient time. Meat is a bad conductor of heat, so that the interior of a large mass only becomes heated very slowly. The necessary time may be determined by experiment, putting the bulb of a thermometer in the centre of the mass, and noting how long it takes to mark 100° C.

Before describing the practical application of the Appert method, we will state its principle. When the hermetically sealed vessel is heated as described all the ferments inside are killed, and one cause of putrefaction is removed. At the same time, however, the oxygen present enters into chemical combination with the food, so that all chemical ferments are prevented from acting. If the heating has not been sufficient for this, the preservation is imperfect, and decomposition will finally set in. That such is the case we have proved by an experiment which we here mention, because it strongly confirms our argument that the presence of free oxygen is conducive to putrefaction in spite of any previous heating. Steamed beef was put into two long-necked glass flasks of equal size, and they were at once closed up by fusing the necks. While, however, in one as much meat as possible was introduced, the other was only one-third filled. Both flasks were immersed in boiling water for six hours, and put away in a cupboard. The contents of the filled flask were perfectly good four years later, and their taste could not be distinguished from that of freshly cooked meat. In the other flask a change was soon visible to the eye. The flesh became gelatinous in appearance. At the end of the four years it was slimy, and absolutely uneatable. After twelve hours' exposure to the air it was completely putrid, although it showed no trace of the presence of any organised ferment at the moment it was taken from the flask. We must here recognise the effect of the presence of a considerable quantity of oxygen. This strives to combine with the meat and produce decompositions which, although not fermentative or putrefactive, are of a closely similar nature, and are quite enough to make the meat uneatable.

In considering the practice of Appert's method, we have first to study the cans. These are either cylinders or four-sided cases.

Although the latter do not waste so much space as the former when packed with others, the cylinders are generally preferred. They are easier to make by machinery than the cases, and much easier to solder up. It is essential that the can should be made of well-tinned sheet iron, and soldered with the greatest care, for the least opening means the putrefaction of the contents. It is also advisable to give the outsides of the cans a good coat of varnish, for if the iron gets laid bare anywhere, it will rust, and an opening be thereby made. The grey varnish may be used, made of soot, levigated chalk, and boiled oil, and must be well made, so as to long remain elastic. If it is carefully applied, cans may be used which are tinned inside only.

In filling the cans care must be taken to pack the meat as closely as possible and to fill the can completely, so that very little air is left inside. The can is soldered up directly it is full, and the cans are then boiled in batches.

It is a troublesome plan to put the cans in a pan, fill it with water and boil for a long enough time, and much heat is wasted in evaporating the water. A better way is to heat by steam. For this purpose the cans are so arranged in a chamber that the steam can circulate freely round each one, the bottom layer of cans resting on a trellis work. The steam enters below this trellis, and escapes at the top of the chamber. A tap is provided below the trellis for drawing off condensed water. At first the steam is admitted at a pressure of two to three atmospheres. When condensation has ceased the blow-off cock is shut, and the passage of steam is continued till all the meat has been heated to 100°C. The time required for this can only be ascertained by experiment, as it depends on the bulk to be heated and the amount and temperature of the steam. Whether steam or boiling water is used, care must be taken to raise the temperature gradually, to give time for the absorption of the oxygen by the flesh. Too rapid heating may also burst the cans, by the sudden expansion of the air in them. The cooled tins should be examined to see if their ends have become somewhat concave. This is a sign that the can has passed through the treatment satisfactorily, for it is caused by the external atmospheric pressure, and denotes a partial vacuum inside the can.

If a can on keeping develops signs of internal pressure, *i.e.*, a tendency of the ends to become less concave or even to bulge out, it is a sign of the putrefaction of the contents, due to imperfect heating and consequent failure to destroy the ferments in them. The bulging is due to the evolution of putrefactive gases.

In large preserving factories the present practice to secure absolute certainty, is to raise the pressure in the steam chamber to three atmospheres at the close of the period known by experience to be enough to heat all the meat to 100°C. This causes a further rise of temperature to about 130°C, and gives full security for the absorption of all oxygen and the death of all ferments.

The Appert process is suitable not only for meat, but for every readily putrefiable substance, such as vegetable matters generally, and also for the preservation of whole fruit in syrup. If glass cans are used, they must be corked air-tight, and heated in water in such a way that the corks do not get wet. To prevent the glass cracking, the heating must be very gradual. When the heating is at an end, fused paraffin is poured over the corks, and the vessels are then allowed to cool in the water. The atmosphere pressure then drives the paraffin into the pores of the cork, and makes a perfectly air-tight stopper,

The chief difficulty in the Appert process is to leave a minimum of air in the tins. The practice has therefore been introduced of driving the air out before the tins are soldered up. This can be done in various ways. When flesh is preserved in its broth, a small hole is blade in the lid of the can after it has been soldered up. This hole is in its turn soldered up when the heating of the can has caused the steam developed inside to expel the air. With large cans they are first tightly filled, and then as much water is put in as possible. The can is then soldered up, a small hole is made in the lid, and the process is continued as above. In opening a tin of preserved meat, careful notice should be taken that the air is heard rushing in when the first puncture is made.

Another rather more troublesome process for getting rid of the air is the following: The cover of the can has a small tube passing through it. While steam is issuing from this during the heating of the can, the tube is closed with a pair of pincers and soldered up.

It has been proposed to put spirit into the can and not to solder the final hole as long as spirit vapour can be ignited at it. It is, however, very difficult to drive off all the spirit, and it imparts a disagreeable taste to the meat. The above processes answer better, with less expense, and without impairing the flavour of the meat.

The use of preserved meat has not become so general in Europe as it deserves to be. One reason is prejudice, and another is the too high prices charged for it. There is, however, no doubt that prices must fall rapidly, as soon as manufacturers can reckon on a large consumption.

Ox and sheep flesh for provisioning ships and fortresses, sardines and tunny-fish in oil, and lobsters, are at present the chief preserved meats; but large factories could easily supply the whole of Europe with flesh of all kinds, almost at the same price as when fresh. No one would then think of making extract of beef out of partridges, as a Russian manufacturer, who exhibited at Vienna in 1873, had done, for the bird would certainly fetch a better price preserved whole.

Valuable as Liebig's extract is, it has not found its way into every household. If in South America the flesh were preserved as such, instead of being worked up into extract, it would be much better for producers and public alike.

In England the use of preserved meat is far more extended than in Germany, as a result of her huge commercial relations with every part of the globe. Part of the English appreciation is, no doubt, learned from the sailors of the nation who have been compelled by circumstances to use and to learn the value of preserved food.

By the Appert process we can preserve every kind of flesh, either boiled or roast, smoked or varnished, with broth or without. The presence of broth helps to drive out the air by the steam it develops on heating.

In preserving large animals the bones are removed to save space, and only flesh is put into the cans. Small animals, such as fowls, are best preserved with the bones. It cannot be too strongly recommended to label the tin with the net weight, and a few directions for use. The following is an example of such a label:

"15 kilos net of boiled beef. Before opening place the tin for .... minutes in boiling water."

The time given must of course depend on the size of the tin. From ten to fifteen minutes suffice for 2-lb. tins.

As a tool is needed for opening the can, the plan has been used of late of fixing the cover on by a metal strip soldered both to the can and its lid. A key is provided whereby this strip can be removed and the lid raised.

Chapter 14

Preserving Flesh by Smoking

The methods already described aim at preserving as far as possible the original character of either raw or cooked meat. Other processes cover the outside of the meat with antiseptics in order to preserve it.

One of these methods is smoking. As already stated the active principles concerned are the creosote or carbolic acid in the wood smoke. A very slight smoky flavour, which properly smoked meat possesses, is agreeable to most people, and the flesh will keep for many months.

The smoking is, however, rarely well done. All that is thought of is to get it over as quickly as possible and to imitate the characteristic reddish brown hue of properly smoked meat by other means. Flesh which has only been smoked just long enough to acquire the characteristic odour, only keeps a very short time, perhaps not more than a week in the summer.

In household smoking the meat is hung in a wide chimney, or in a special smoke chamber with which several chimneys communicate. The joints are first rubbed with brine, and are hung so that they do not touch one another. To prevent them from being blackened, it is a good plan to wrap them in paper.

It is absolutely essential that no smoke reaches the meat except from fires of hard wood, such as beech or oak. The smoke of coal or turf contains substances which make the meat quite uneatable; and that from resinous woods, such as pine and fir, gives the flesh an unpleasant resinous taste. Care must be taken that the meat is far enough from the fire to avoid all risk of fusing the fat.

During the smoking the flesh contracts and becomes more solid by losing water, and becomes of a rich dark reddish brown on the outside as it acquires the smoky flavour.

Large pieces, such as hams, require several weeks' smoking, for the effect must penetrate the meat completely. It is, however, possible to shorten this time considerably by proper arrangements.

We recommend for smoking on a large scale the arrangement represented in Figure 11. The fire H communicates with the smoking-room R by a chimney several yards long. The lower room containing the fire may conveniently be a cellar, and the smoking-room on the ground floor. The opening of the chimney in the floor is surrounded by an iron ring about six inches high, which compels the smoke to distribute itself among the pieces of meat which are hung up in rows, with room between each pair of rows for a man to pass. At the corner of the room farthest from the opening in the floor, an opening for the escape of the smoke is provided, E.

The pieces of meat should be so hung that the largest pieces get the smoke first, while small articles, such as sausages, are hung nearest the exit.

When all the meat is hung, the door of the room is shut and the fire is made with thin sticks or, preferably, with shavings of hard wood in a slightly damp state. Beech gives the most creosote, so it should always be used whenever it can be got. At the same time that the fire is lit in H a bundle of straw is kindled in the lower part of E to make a draught. When this has been started, it will continue to carry the smoke through the smoking-room without any more straw being burnt. The damper S serves to prevent the combustion in H

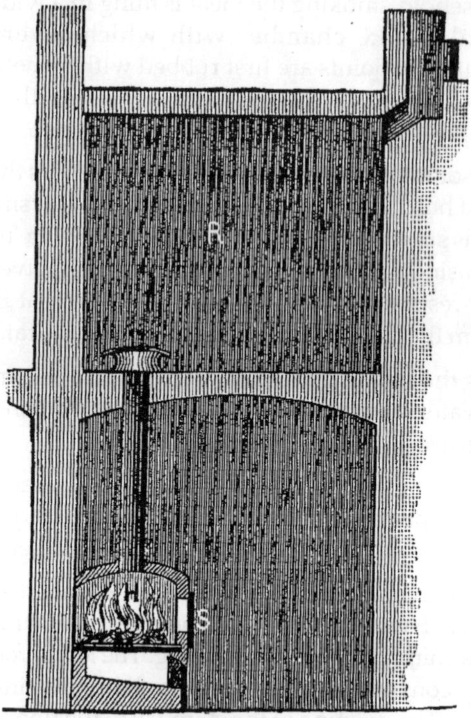

Figure 11

from becoming too vigorous, and thus ensures a smoky fire. The object of having a long iron chimney is to cool the smoke before it reaches the meat, as it must never fuse the fat. At the start the damper may be left fairly wide open, as the cold meat cools the smoke. As it gets warm, however, the damper is gradually closed more and more, so that the flame may be smoky but not sooty. It is a very good plan to have the door of the smoking-room glazed, so that a view of a thermometer hanging up inside may be had. The temperature of the room must not be allowed to exceed 40°C. When the process is finished, the fire is allowed to go out and the damper is opened wide. The air of the smoking-room will very soon free from smoke, and the meat can then be taken out.

With a well-regulated fire this arrangement completes the process fairly quickly, the time required for a large room averaging about a week. The time required and the loss of weight undergone by the meat have caused the invention of other processes, distinguished by the name of quick-smoking.

Chapter 15
Quick-Smoking

The foundation of this process is the fact that raw pyroligneous acid, obtained by the dry distillation of wood, contains creosote as well as acetic acid and water. It has a strong smoky smell, and has powerful antiseptic properties.

It is used for quick-smoking by dipping the meat into it for a few seconds, draining it, and then hanging up. As soon as the meat has absorbed the acid, it is redipped two or three times, and finally left for from thirty to sixty hours, according to the size of the piece. By that time the process is complete. The dipping solution is made by diluting the pyroligneous acid with twice its volume of water, and both the solution and the room in which the work is done should be just warm enough merely to soften the fat, whereby the absorption of the acid is made more rapid.

To give the cured meat a taste of juniper a little juniper oil is dissolved in the pyroligneous acid before it is diluted. The following proportions answer extremely well:

Pyroligneous acid	100 gallons
Water	200 gallons
Juniper oil	5 gallons

Most of the acetic acid present disappears from the meat by evaporation, and it is better and cheaper to use a mixture which contains proportionately less pyroligneous acid. An excellent recipe for the solution for soaking the meat is as follows:

Water	100 gallons
Pyroligneous acid	10 gallons
Creosote	1 gallon
Juniper oil	1 gallon

The creosote is first dissolved in the acid, and the oil is then added. The acid is then poured into the water in a thin stream with constant stirring.

Very quick smoking can be done with the smoking-room above described by placing on the floor shallow dishes filled from a mixture of 10 gallons of pyroligneous acid, 10 gallons of water, and 2 gallons of creosote. A large bath sponge is put in each dish to facilitate the evaporation of the creosote and acid.

Yet another quite different method is to collect the soot from the chimneys of fires where only wood is burnt, and to boil it with ten times its weight of water for about half an hour. Then filter, and add to the solution 5 per cent of salt. Hang the meat to be preserved in this solution, which contains the creosote from the soot, for from one to twenty hours, according to its size. Thin sausages need only half an hour, but large hams require fully twenty hours. This process gives a better taste than the processes in which artificially prepared creosote is used.

Chapter 16

Preserving Meat with Salt

Beginning with the old salting processes, we find when we consider the nature of meat that they are very wasteful.

Flesh consists of muscular fibre containing in solution large quantities of the nourishing constituents of the meat, albuminoids of various kinds, creatine, phosphates etc. Muscular fibrin itself is of comparatively small value as a food, and flesh which has been thoroughly exhausted with water, is unwillingly eaten even by hungry dogs. Now pickling in brine effects a substitution in the meat of salt water for these nourishing liquids which it formerly contained, so that the meat becomes of very little nutritive value, the valuable parts of it going into the brine. Besides, what is left of the meat is rendered very indigestible. It is no wonder that now a days salt meat is in small favour, although meat can be preserved by salt without any of the above drawbacks.

Salting is generally done by dipping the meat in water, then rolling it in powdered salt, and then packing it as closely as possible in a cask. On the lowest layer of pieces salt is scattered, mixed with pepper, bay, or juniper. When the cask is nearly full the contents are covered with a piece of wood loaded with weights. In the cask the salt abstracts water from the meat, and forms with it brine, which penetrates the flesh, replacing the liquids it formerly contained. It is a very good plan to fill up the cask with brine from the start. To keep the red colour of the flesh, saltpetre is also added in quantities up to 5 per cent. The sodium saltpetre–Chili saltpetre–will not do. Only the potassium nitrate must be used. All the processes which have been proposed instead of this antiquated one are directed to saving as much of the nutritive elements as possible, and to effect the process in a few minutes. Various plans have been tried, on similar principles to those which at present govern the preservation of wood, by soaking it with antiseptics. The salt is driven into the meat by atmospheric or water pressure.

Chapter 17

Quick-Salting by Air-Pressure

The apparatus used for this is represented in Figure 12. *C* is a cylinder of thick iron plate, tinned inside, the top of the cylinder is flanged for an indiarubber washer, by means of which a lid can be screwed on air-tight. From the cover the two tubes *R* and R_1 pass, and can be closed by the taps shown. *R* communicates with an air-pump, and R_1 dips into *S*, which contains a sufficient quantity of concentrated brine. The tube R_1 proceeding from the bottom of the cylinder, serves to draw off liquid from it. A short safety tube with a cock is shown at *H*.

When the cylinder has been packed with meat as closely as possible, the cover is screwed on, and all cocks are shut except that in *R*. A vacuum is then made with the air-pump. When the pump gauge shows that there is a good vacuum in *C*, the communication with the air-pump is closed, and the tap in *R* is opened. The external pressure then drives the brine into *C*. After five or ten minutes the cocks at *H* and R_2 are opened, and the brine is run off for use again.

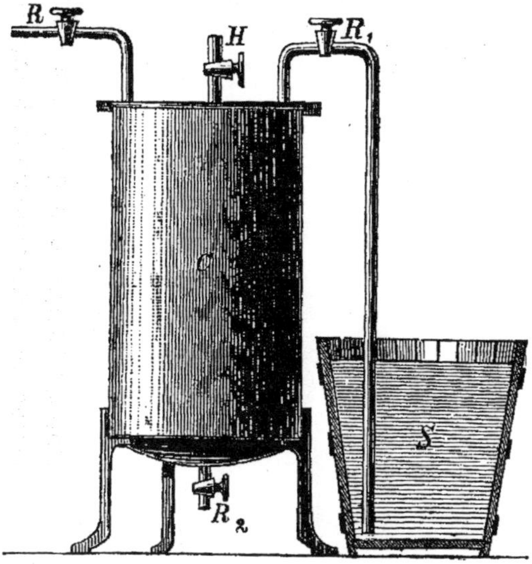

Figure 12

The cover is then removed and the meat taken out and hung in an airy room. As soon as it is dry, which happens even with large pieces in a few days, it is packed in cases for transport. It keeps much better than meat salted in the usual way.

Saltpetre is added to the brine used, and any aromatic bodies that may be judged desirable. The latter are packed in powder in a linen bag, which is then hung in the brine for a few days before it is used. Or the spices may be soaked for a few days in strong vinegar, which is then added to the brine. The short duration of this process prevents any substitution by the brine of the natural fluids of the meat. The brine is simply added to them. Thus the meat is preserved while retaining its nutritive properties.

It must be remembered in filling the cylinder that when the vacuum is made, the expansion of the air confined in the meat makes it swell considerably. Room must of course be allowed for this.

In working on a very large scale with a battery of cylinders, the range is so managed that the process is worked continuously and in regular order.

It is very convenient to make C swing on trunnions. *R* and R_1 are then made of indiarubber with a wire spiral inside to prevent the external pressure from flattening them.

Chapter 18

Quick-Salting by Liquid-Pressure

This process has the advantage of requiring very simple apparatus only, and it is specially applicable to the preservation of large masses. A reservoir of concentrated brine is on a high level, say on the roof of a house, of at least thirty feet above the room where the process is worked. A pipe brought down from the reservoir is connected by a length of indiarubber tube with the iron pointed tube shown in Figure 13. This pipe is about eight inches long, is provided with a tap, and has numerous holes bored in it towards the point. If this point is inserted into the middle of a piece of flesh and the tap is opened, the hydrostatic pressure causes the salt water to penetrate the flesh completely in a very few minutes. The pieces impregnated in this way are placed for about twenty-four hours in concentrated brine, and the meat loses no nutritive matter, as it is already thoroughly penetrated with brine. The pieces are then simply dried or slightly smoked.

A whole carcass of an ox can be salted very quickly by the injection process used by anatomists. The beast is slaughtered by

Figure 13

severing the spinal cord in the neck. Its chest is then opened and the heart lifted out, without, however, injuring the vessels. The blood is then drained away by making an incision in each ventricle. An iron pipe is then inserted through the left ventricle into the aorta and tied firmly into it. Concentrated brine is then pumped through the pipe. The brine will penetrate every part of the circulatory system down to the finest capillaries, and drive out all the remaining blood, which begins to pour out in a few seconds after the commencement of the pumping. Another minute's pumping after all bleeding has ceased will finish the salting. The carcass is cut up as usual, and the pieces are laid in concentrated brine for twenty-four hours and hung up in the air to dry. It can then, if wished, be smoked by any of the processes above described.

Other antiseptics have been proposed as substitutes for salt in the processes of which we are just now treating. There is no advantage to be gained by using them, for none of them are cheaper or more effective than salt, and no one knows what action they have on our digestive organs. Those chiefly advocated are the bisulphites of soda and lime, used by the air-pressure process. In one proposed method, after the forcing of the bisulphite solution into the meat, the air is again pumped out, and carbonic acid is allowed to act on the meat, whereby it is said to keep better.

It is certainly true that meat can be kept good for several weeks by giving it ten minutes' immersion in a solution of salt and bisulphite of soda, and thereafter dipping it again for a few seconds every day, for sodium bisulphite is as powerful an antiseptic as sulphurous acid itself.

A mixture of salt and sugar, in the proportion of 1 lb. of the former to 4 lb. of the latter, will preserve meat. According to Wohly, who has tried the method, the meat is rubbed with the mixture, then left for two days, and finally pressed and packed in a cask, which is then filled up with fused fat.

Chapter 19

Gamgee's Method of Preserving Meat

The object of Gamgee's method is the preservation of meat in the raw state. It depends on the joint action of sulphurous acid and carbon monoxide without any salting. As both these gases are antiseptic, the process deserves attention.

Gamgee proposes to make the animal insensible by causing it to inhale carbon monoxide, and then to slaughter and cut it up as quickly as possible, packing the meat immediately in air-tight vessels. The vessels may be of wood or of brick-work rendered in cement. Through their covers passes a tube, which opens under a grate in a cast-iron cylinder. The part of the cylinder above the grate is packed with red-hot coke. Another pipe leads from the top of this cylinder to the bottom of the flesh-receptacle. By means of a pump the air in the meat-receptacle is forced through the hot coke and back into the receptacle, and is kept so circulating till all its oxygen is converted into carbon monoxide. The action of sulphurous acid is then started. Before the cover of the meat-receptacle is fastened down, a box containing wood charcoal, saturated with sulphurous acid, by exposing it in a freshly burnt state to that gas, is placed in it. When all the oxygen present has been converted into carbon monoxide, the charcoal box is opened by pulling a string without opening the meat-receptacle. The sulphurous acid then escapes from the charcoal, being replaced by part of the carbon monoxide. The meat is then left for nine or ten days in the mixed atmosphere of sulphurous acid and carbon monoxide.

If meat so preserved is hung up in a dry place, it will keep for weeks, even in the summer, and if the additional precaution is taken of dipping it in a solution of gelatine before hanging it up, it will keep for months without the least change.

Chapter 20

The Preservation of Eggs

Eggs are a food of very great importance, as they contain, to a higher degree even than meat, all the nutritive elements in such proportions as are required for the nourishment of the body. In those countries where the winter is fairly severe, the hens leave off laying during the cold weather. It is therefore necessary to preserve the eggs, which the extremely great putrescibility of their soluble albumen makes very difficult.

Eggs consist of three parts: shell, white, and yolk. The two latter are intended as food for the embryo. The shell is very porous, and admits the air necessary for the respiration of the embryo. As it gives out carbon through the pores in the form of carbon dioxide, but receives nothing from without, the egg gets lighter and lighter, as incubation proceeds. The inside of the shell is lined with a very fine membrane.

The white consists of a very concentrated solution of sodium albumen in water, enclosed in large transparent walled cells, which cause the white to form a continuous mass. The yolk also contains albumen and a large quantity of fat in the form of an emulsion, and also phosphoric acid, sugar, and some other substances with which we are less well acquainted.

That an egg while being incubated by the hen does not putrefy, is due to the constant expiration of carbonic acid by the developing organism of the embryo, carbonic acid being an antiseptic. When an egg is about to be used as food, no germ can be developing, but such an egg is dead and incapable of resisting the attacks of destructive influences.

When an egg is left to itself, water evaporates through the pores, and air enters by them, bringing with it the spores of ferments, which find a perfect food in the white and yolk, and develop rapidly at their expense.

Therefore the best method of preserving eggs is to prevent air from entering through the pores of the shell. This must of course be done while the egg is quite fresh. Once decomposition has begun, all the exclusion of air can do is to make it proceed more slowly. The putrefactive gases, too, finally burst the shell. We must therefore choose eggs for preservation with great care, and it is best to preserve the eggs when they are known to be new laid.

Lime water is largely used for preserving eggs. Fresh slaked lime dissolves in twenty times its weight of water to a clear solution, which greedily absorbs carbon dioxide from the air, and becomes covered with a scum of carbonate of lime. The action of lime water in preserving eggs depends on the same thing. An egg when wetted with lime water, gets the pores of its shell filled with carbonate of lime on exposure to the air, and thus the ingress of germs is prevented. Concentrated lime water should be kept ready in a vat which has some slaked lime always on the bottom, and is stirred up occasionally. If, however, the eggs are not dipped several times, some of the pores may escape being stopped up.

Many other substances are used besides lime water, and these act in the same way. Dextrine and boiled oil have both been used. We have found that a solution of colophony in turpentine, mixed with as much spirit as it would bear without precipitation, answered welt. The coating is very thin and uniform. Solution of indiarubber can also be used. Another good way is to dip the eggs into gelatine solution at a temperature of 40°C, then dry them, and dip them for ten minutes into a solution of tannin. The pores thus become stopped up with leather.

A very excellent and very cheap plan is to dip the eggs in waterglass and then dry them. The silica of the waterglass is set free by the carbon dioxide of the air, and then forms with the lime of the egg-shell a glassy sheet of calcium silicate, which closes all the pores. We can testify that eggs preserved in this will keep perfectly fresh for months. The eggs should be kept immersed in the solution for about ten minutes by floating a board on the top of them. They are then removed and stood up with their small ends in little holes in a shelf for two days. The eggs can then be packed for storage or transit. There is an additional advantage attending this process, at least for eggs which are to be sent long distances, in that the shell becomes much stronger and less liable to breakage.

As eggs cannot go bad without oxygen, they may be kept for a long time in powdered charcoal, which, however, has to be renewed at least once a month.

Glycerine is an excellent preservative for eggs. A mixture of glycerine with half its volume of water is made, and the eggs are placed in it and kept below the surface by a floating piece of wood. The same solution will serve for constant use for a long time, other eggs being put in when some are removed. To preserve the solution as a stock bath, only clean eggs must be put in the glycerine.

Chapter 21

Preservation of White and Yolk of Egg

Egg-albumen is used for many technical purposes. Both egg-albumen and blood-albumen are used in calico-printing (for pigments), and the yolks of the eggs used may advantageously be preserved. Moreover, the albumen needs to be preserved if it has to be kept in stock for even a short time. Either can be preserved by simple drying, however. The first thing to be attended to is to get yolk and white quite separate. Each is then beaten to break up the cell walls, and spread out in a thin layer, usually of a polished sheet of iron or of glass. They are then dried in a current of air at a temperature not exceeding 60° C., or the albumen will become insoluble, and can then be detached in dry plates. The yolk has too much fat in it ever to become so rigid as the albumen does.

Chapter 22
Milk-Preservation

Milk is an important food, especially for children, but is peculiarly liable to decomposition. In the summer, when thunder is about, milk will turn in a few hours after it is drawn from the cow. Another reason makes the transport of milk to great distances very difficult. The constant shaking separates the milk. These circumstances put great difficulties in the way of the use of milk in large towns, and incite to adulteration with water or other substances which delay curdling.

In many places, like Switzerland for example, the production of milk is overwhelmingly greater than the consumption. Hence the price is very low, and the milk has to be made into cheese and butter in order to make it pay. In large towns, on the contrary, the price is so high that the milk-producers could make larger profits by selling the milk there in a preserved state, at prices which would make their milk come a little cheaper than the uncondensed article.

The curdling of milk is caused by the conversion of the milk-sugar into lactic acid by a ferment. When the milk is thus made acid, its casein, which is dissolved while the liquid is in its normally alkaline state, is precipitated. By adding small quantities of borax or carbonate of potash, the acidification of the milk may be delayed a little, but such additions are inadvisable from a sanitary point of view, and they are forbidden in most countries.

Two ways of preserving milk are known: one with, one without, the abstraction of its water. In the first case we have *condensed*, in the second *preserved*, milk. When the milk is intended for transport to comparatively short distances, and it is therefore unnecessary to save the cost of the freight of the water, it appears best to preserve the milk by Appert's process. In this case the milk is filled which fresh drawn into iron cans. The cover is first soldered down, but a funnel is fixed in a hole in the cover. The tin is filled through the funnel until the milk reaches the upper end of the funnel tube, which is soldered into the cover and projects about four inches above it. The funnel is next partly filled with pieces of pure paraffin, and the tin is kept in water nearly boiling for one or two hours. It is then allowed to cool to about 50° C., and closed air-tight at that temperature, by squeezing up the tube with pincers and then soldering it up.

Milk treated in this way contains no living ferment, and is shut up air-tight. Hence, like all foods preserved by Appert's process, it keeps unchanged almost indefinitely. The can should be turned over several times before being opened, to mix it, as the cream of course rises to the top.

It is, however, undeniable that this preserved milk, although it cannot be altered by ferments, yet develops a slightly bitter after-taste. The cause of this is unknown.

The Appert process is unsuitable for milk which has to be sent great distances, on account of the waste of space and freightage involved in forwarding the water, although it seems to us very suitable for the supply of large towns from neighbouring milk-producing districts. The vessels which have contained preserved milk can generally be used again.

Chapter 22
Condensed Milk

In the evaporation of milk, a scum of casein forms on the surface, which greatly hinders the escape of the steam. This scum usually also adheres to the sides of the evaporating vessel and gives the milk a burnt taste. The burning can be avoided by evaporation on a water-bath, so that the evaporating vessel is always below 100° C., but the milk always clots. The remedy for both evils is evaporation in a vacuum pan. Here it is possible to boil milk at a temperature of about 50° C.

If the milk is not to be evaporated at once, it must be kept as cool as possible until it goes into the vacuum pan, to prevent it from going sour. A very good plan is to pour the milk into shallow tin plate pans, and to blow air, previously cooled by ice, over the surface. On a large scale, refrigerating apparatus is used to cool the air.

The first step in making condensed milk is to boil the milk in an open pan, to kill all the ferments in air. It is then run hot into the vacuum pan, which is then set in action, the milk being heated by a steam-coil. The degree of vacuum is arranged so that the milk boils at between 50° and 60° C. In about three hours the milk is reduced to a quarter of its original volume, but fresh milk may be supplied to the pan as the process goes on. The condensed milk is fed hot into the cans, which are soldered as soon as full.

In the factories of the Anglo-Swiss Condensed Milk Co., brown sugar is added to the milk before it goes to the vacuum pan. The result is that when the condensed milk is diluted with water, the resulting liquid has a very sweet taste, which many people do not like.

We consider this addition of sugar entirely superfluous. All that is needed is to evaporate the milk to one-fourth of its bulk. So long as the can is unopened the milk will keep unchanged. If it is opened and the contents are not touched, the upper part of the milk dries to a horny crust, which protects the liquid below from decomposition. Even if this crust is constantly broken up, no lactic acid is formed for five or six days, and the large quantities of sugar and salts present cause it to be produced very slowly.

Anyone who lives in a large town knows to what an extent milk is adulterated, and will learn to appreciate condensed milk when once it has been given a trial. We are convinced that the best profit is obtained where milk is produced on a large scale, by condensing it. The soldered metal tins are best for sending condensed milk long distances, but for milk which has to travel only short journeys, glass bottles do quite well, provided they are filled with good sound corks.

Chapter 24

The Preservation of Fat

If it were not for the almost insuperable difficulties in the way of obtaining fats in a pure state, there would not be much to say about their preservation. Simple exclusion of air would be sufficient.

The decomposition of fats is invariably accompanied by the production of small amounts of free acid, which, in spite of its relatively small quantity, makes the fat so repulsive in smell and taste as to be uneatable. The inhabitants of the Arctic zone, however, are said to prefer rancid to fresh fat. We can gather from this that even very low temperatures will not keep fat sweet. Payer mentions that the butter of the Austrian North Pole expedition became so rancid as to be uneatable.

The decomposition of fat is probably started by the traces of albuminous liquid which it always contains. We believe that the pleasant taste of fat which we designate as absolutely fresh, depends upon incipient rancidity, and base our opinion on the fact that we have observed that perfectly fresh-made butter has a slightly acid taste when it contains buttermilk, and that butter quite free from buttermilk has no taste whatever when just made, and contains no trace of free acid. A few days' exposure to the air in thin slices gives, however, this butter the characteristic taste and smell, the appearance of which is invariably attended with the formation of traces of acid.

To preserve solid fat it is treated with very dilute sulphuric acid or caustic soda to destroy the foreign matter present. To perform the same office for liquid fats, concentrated sulphuric acid is used. Such treatment, however, cannot be adopted with fats to be used as food, and recourse must be had to fusing the fat or to drying it. In the last case, however, the salt added affects the taste.

Butter-Preservation

To keep butter fresh we know no better plan than to squeeze it thoroughly, so as to get all the buttermilk out of it, and then to pack it in large pieces with ice all round it. It will then keep for weeks so fresh that the most sensitive tongue will be unable to detect any unpleasant taste in it.

The Melting of Butter

To keep butter for longer periods, it is melted and poured into wooden tubs or, better, into large stoneware pots. This process is, however, often carried out so carelessly that fatty acids are formed by the fusion, this being the result of over-heating by a naked fire. Butter, like all fats, is a very poor conductor of heat, and the temperature employed is often far more than enough to melt the butter.

The following process, however, preserves butter well, without making its taste or smell different from those of the fresh article.

Perfectly fresh butter is put into a cylindrical vessel standing in water. The water is then heated to about 40°C., and all the butter is soon fused. As soon as this has happened, the water is raised to the boil as quickly as possible. The albuminous bodies in the butter then coagulate and rise as a scum, which is removed as it forms. When no more scum rises, the water is allowed to go off the boil, but is kept hot enough for another half-hour to keep the butter melted for the buttermilk to settle to the bottom. The butter is then, while still liquid, ladled out into stoneware pots. These are placed in ice, and when the butter has set, it is covered with about half an inch of paraffin just hot enough to be poured.

If the butter to be preserved is not quite fresh, it is fused with 10 per cent of its weight with 1 per cent caustic soda lye and thoroughly stirred. The rest of the process is exactly as above described. The lye neutralises the fatty acids and carries them down into the buttermilk at the bottom of the cylindrical vessel. Other fats, such as lard, can be treated exactly as here described for butter.

SALTING BUTTER

The preservation of butter by salt is a very common process, more so, however, in the North than in the South. Various amounts of salt are added, according to the intended use of the butter. Table butter contains about 1 per cent of salt, cooking butter 2 per cent, or more. To mix the butter and the salt as intimately as possible, the butter is rolled out, strewn with the salt, and then kneaded till the salt is no longer visible, and every part of the mass has the same taste. Many people recommend kneading in the salt in two halves, the two kneadings taking place about twenty-four hours apart.

A machine for salting butters is shown in Figure 14. This machine reduces the butter to ribbons, which are sprinkled with

Figure 14

salt, bunched up, and passed again through the machine. This process is repeated several times.

Salt butter is best packed in stoneware, being pressed well in so as to leave no vacant spaces. When the vessel is full the butter is carefully levelled off and strewn with salt, so as to cover the butter completely.

Tubs for storing salt butter should be soaked for several weeks before use, best in running water, to remove the resinous matter from the wood, to prevent the taste of the butter, which like all fats greedily absorbs odouriferous or strongly tasting bodies, from being spoiled by them. Tubs which have been used, are washed out thoroughly with hot soda and water, and can then be filled again.

Up to now we have been concerned with the preservation of meat and other animal produces in as far as possible their original condition. There are, however, numerous preparations classed with preserved animal matter, in which other things are mixed and preserved with the animal product.

Examples of this kind of preparation are soup-tablets, meat-biscuits, and extract of meat. As these preparations are of real importance as articles of food, and obtain a continually increasing sale, we must consider them in some detail.

Chapter 25
Manufacture of Soup-Tablets

These tablets are intended to produce soup when dissolved in hot water. Some tablets on the market do this, and some do not.

The first step in the manufacture is to extract the soluble matters from meat. To do this the meat must not be plunged into boiling water. If this is done, the outside of the meat is made impervious by the coagulation of the albumen in it, and even long boiling then fails to do more than very imperfectly extract the soluble constituents of the meat. The proper plan is to steep the meat in cold water, and then to heat up very gradually, and not to a sufficient temperature to coagulate the albumen.

In the manufacture of soup-tablets, the meat is scrupulously freed from fat before treatment. It is then minced in a mincing machine, or chopped up small with a chopper, and steeped in not too hard water, which is gradually brought to a temperature not exceeding 60° C. The heating is kept up with constant stirring (for which mechanical rousers are needed in working on a large scale) for several hours. The proportion of water to meat should be two parts to one by weight, and at the end of three hours nothing will be left undissolved but worthless fibrin. After the first three hours, the temperature is raised to about 90° C. The liquid, previously clear, then becomes thick, and a scum rises to its surface. Both these appearances are due to the coagulation of the albumen. The liquid can now be kept by filling vessels quite full with it while still hot and then closing them air-tight. It will then keep for many months, and the process can be recommended for preserving broth in the household.

To make soup-tablets from the liquid, it is mixed with about 1 lb. of salt for every 100 lb. of meat used, and filtered through several folds of linen. The filtrate is evaporated down in very shallow tin plate pans, without, however, allowing it to boil, till a sample sets hard when cold. The whole mass is then cast into moulds. Properly made soup-tablets are usually of a pale brown colour and transparent, and give a perfectly clear solution in water, having the taste of fresh beef-tea.

Sham Soup-Tablets

These consist almost entirely of gelatine, and their nutritive value is very small. The sale of this article has done much harm to the trade in the legitimate tablet, which really is nutritious.

To make so-called soup-tablets of the better kind, chopped calves' feet and trotters are treated as above described, but at a boiling heat continued for several hours, which converts into gelatine everything capable of conversion into that substance. The liquid is coloured with burnt sugar before moulding, to give the colour of the genuine tablets. To cover the insipidity of the gelatine, herbs and salt are added before the solution is filtered.

These products are not so absolutely worthless as certain French tablets, which are made from manufactured gelatine and not directly from animal products of any kind. These articles contain nothing but gelatine, burnt sugar, and herb extracts, and to sell them as soup-tablets is undoubtedly a fraud.

Soup-tablets are very hygroscopic, and hence very apt to mould. They must therefore be kept in air-tight cases.

Chapter 26
Meat-Biscuits

These are an American invention very suitable for shipping and military purposes. A broth is made as directed for genuine soup-tablets, and evaporated to a third of its bulk. It is then mixed with flour to a paste, which is moulded and baked to a light brown colour.

The proportions of the constituents vary, but as a rule the flour used is double the weight of the meat for the broth. The biscuits are flavoured with spices to relieve their insipidity.

Meat-biscuits are made by Calamand of Paris by boiling 1020 lb. of joints of beef with 100 gallons of water for four hours. During the cooking a bag containing 400 lb. of vegetables, together with salt, pepper, etc., is hung in the broth. After the four hours the bones are removed and the meat is cut up, and the boiling is then continued till the volume is down to 45 gallons. 180 oz. of sugar, for preserving purposes, and 2000 lb. of flour, are next added, and the paste is finally moulded and baked in masses weighing about 120 lb. each, the percentage composition of which is as follows:

Dry flour	76.5
Dry meat	5.8

Fat	6.3
Dry vegetables	2.8
Spices and sugar	0.9
Water	7.7

It is not necessary to keep closely to the above recipe to get a product as good as Calamand's. The proportions of from 25 to 30 lb. of meat to from 48 to 50 lb. of flour give equally excellent results. The higher the percentage of meat, the greater the nutritive value of the biscuit. To preserve the biscuits they should be dipped hot from the oven in a hot solution of sugar and dextrine, and then dried at a gentle heat, so as to give them a protective coating.

Corned Beef

This American product is destined to take an important place among preserved foods. It is prepared by Appert's method. The meat is freed from fat and cut into slices. These are then packed closely, interestratified with a little salt into cans having a truncated pyramidal shape. The cooking is done with high-pressure steam, and causes the slices to cohere into a solid mass. The taste is excellent in every way, and the article could be made profitably in every country rich in oxen, such as South Russia, Romania, or Hungary.

Chapter 27
Extract of Beef

For the sake of completeness we intend to describe the preparation of this product briefly, although we are aware that its manufacture in Western Europe is impossible on account of the price of the meat. It can only be carried out in countries where they can afford to slaughter cattle for the hide and tallow, *i.e.* in certain parts of Australia and South America. There are meat-extract factories at Montevideo, Texas, and at Fray Bentos in Uruguay (the oldest place of production), and several in Australia.

We owe the introduction of this product and the erection of the first factory, which is at Fray Bentos, to Liebig.

The meat from the cattle of the grass plains of the pampas is freed from bones and fat, and minced. The paste is mixed with water and subjected to great hydraulic pressure. The concentrated solution of the soluble constituents of the meat thus obtained is at once boiled to coagulate the albumen. The clear liquid is then evaporated in vacuum pans, till the mass on cooling has the well-known semi-solid consistency.

When prepared in this way, the extract contains no gelatine, and makes a perfectly clear solution with water. The absence of gelatine and fat makes the extract so unalterable, that a pot of it can be left for as long as desired in a damp mouldy room without undergoing change. All the spores which fall on it are starved to death. According to the makers, 1 lb. of extract is got from 32 lb. of flesh.

Chapter 28

The Preservation of Vegetables Foods in General

The processes here are very closely allied to those for preserving meat. All the processes already described can be employed for vegetables. Vegetables, like flesh, contain carbon, hydrogen, nitrogen, and oxygen, and sometimes, although more rarely than is the case with animal food, sulphur as well. Vegetables also contain mineral salts and water, often enormous amounts of the latter. Cucumbers and water-melons may contain as much as 99 per cent of water.

The chief carbohydrate in vegetable matter is cellulose, which occurs in all young plants, and is the chief constituent of wood. It forms the basis of vegetable tissue, as fibrin does that of flesh. Cellulose (of which cotton affords an example in a nearly pure state) is an extremely permanent substance. Rolls of papyrus are often still in good condition although thousands of years old.

Many other carbohydrates occur in plants, besides cellulose. The chief of these are the various sugars, gums, and vegetable gelatine, ethereal oils, resins, many colouring matters, and the vegetable acids, such as tartaric, malic, benzoic, and tannic. These non-nitrogenous bodies in plants far exceed the nitrogenous compounds in quantity, whereas the contrary is the case in animal matter.

Nevertheless, nitrogenous bodies occur in every part of a plant, and especially in the seed, where they serve to nourish the embryo. They have a close resemblance in their properties to what in flesh we call the albuminoids. Like these they coagulate on heating, and like them they are very putrescible. They are fewer in number than the animal albuminoids, and the chief of them are gluten and vegetable casein.

Gluten, starch, and salts, especially phosphates, constitute the largest part of flour. Pure gluten is a pale brown viscid mass, which readily putrefies. Vegetable casein is especially abundant in the various leguminous seeds, and gives beans and peas their high nutritive value. Like milk casein it is precipitated from solution by acids.

Together with these important bodies we find in many plants, such as tea, coffee, pepper, etc., special nitrogenous bodies called alkaloids. These are more or less poisonous, and are not foods in the proper sense of the term. Their special action on the nerves, however, endows them with so much importance, that it can be said without exaggeration that modern civilisation could not exist without them.

In general, vegetable foods contain constituents more stable than any which occur in animal tissue. Hence vegetable foods are easier to preserve than meat. Again, vegetable foods usually contain less water than animal foods. The reverse is the case in fresh fruit and certain vegetables, but, on the other hand, corn and seed fruits contain less than meat. This, again, makes preservation more easy, and in many cases mere drying is a sufficient preservative process.

At the present day, a combination of the tastes of sugar and of meat is not favoured, so that sugar is rarely used for the preservation of meat or eggs. With vegetables, however, the case is entirely different. Many of them naturally contain large amounts of sugar, and in any case sugar forms an excellent preservative for all vegetables. Alcohol, which cannot be used at all for meat, and acetic acid, which is only applicable to a few kinds of flesh, are also much used for preserving vegetables.

The Preservation of Green Vegetables

These vegetables are a very important part of our daily food, and can only be obtained fresh at certain seasons of the year. We are well aware that they can be grown in greenhouses at any time, but we know equally well that forcing house green-stuff has little more than the appearance of the real thing. It has, as a rule, none of the characteristic taste or dietetic properties of that grown in the open, for the artificial heat is unable to produce the necessary substances. Hence it is of great importance to inhabitants of northern countries to have methods for preserving vegetables in an unchanged state for considerable periods. These processes consist in a great degree of drying and compressing the vegetable matter.

Chapter 29
Compressing Green Vegetables

This is done by abstracting a certain amount of water by heat and then subjecting the vegetables to hydraulic pressure.

All green vegetables can be preserved in this way. The best plants are chosen, and carefully washed and freed from woody parts as when required for immediate consumption. They are then dried in a current of warm air. In Masson's original process the temperature of this air was about 48° C., but our experience shows that 60°C. is a much better temperature, not so much because it accelerates the drying, but because it is high enough to kill the ferment spores in the vegetables, and also facilitates preservation by coagulating the vegetable-albumen.

The vegetables are spread out in the drying-room, either on wicker-work or on perforated plates. The draught through the room can be obtained either with a fan or by means of a high chimney. To enable the work to go on uninterruptedly as long as fresh vegetables are available, it is convenient to have two drying-rooms, one to be in use while the other is being filled or emptied. In very large factories, four are kept always going. The hot air can be turned from one room to the other by means of a valve. To keep up the temperature to the proper degree, the shelves should be as numerous as possible, so as to get the maximum amount of vegetables into the minimum amount of space. The best, cheapest, and strongest shelves are made of a trellis-work of planed laths, covered over with a thin netting. The size of the meshes of this net is proportionate to that of the vegetables to be dried. Many kinds of shelves either take up too much room or are of insufficient strength.

When a fan is not used, the drying-room is supplied with hot air from a coke oven. This is jacketed, so that air is heated in passing through the jacket, and passes thence by two pipes into the drying-room. The outlet pipe passes from the ceiling of the drying-room to the chimney, which creates the necessary draught. Thus the products of combustion from the oven do not enter the drying-room. The openings through which the hot air passes into the drying-room should be closed with a fixed perforated plate, over which a rotatable perforated plate is arranged, in such a way that the ingress of the air may be regulated or entirely shut off by moving the upper plate. The outlet pipe should have a similar arrangement.

A thermometer must 'be hung up in the drying-room, about half-way between the floor and the ceiling, in such a position that the temperature can be seen through a glass window in the door.

A very good drying-room is represented in Figure 15. The oven H stands in the cellar K, and delivers the hot air through an opening O into the drying-room T. The outlet at S is provided with a damper. The air should be sent in very hot at first, say at 100° C., with the entering openings full open, and the exit half-closed. A full supply of heat is necessary at first to get the temperature quickly up to 60°C. When this has been reached, the supply of hot air is lessened so as to maintain without exceeding it. On the average, twenty-four hours in the drying-room dries the vegetables enough, but the time necessarily varies a good deal with different vegetables.

It is unnecessary for preservation to remove all the water. Complete drying, moreover, wastes time and fuel, and prevents any satisfactory pressing afterwards. If too dry the vegetables go to powder in the press, which is very undesirable.

When the vegetables have shrunk a great deal, but are not yet brittle, the desired point has been reached, and they go to the press,

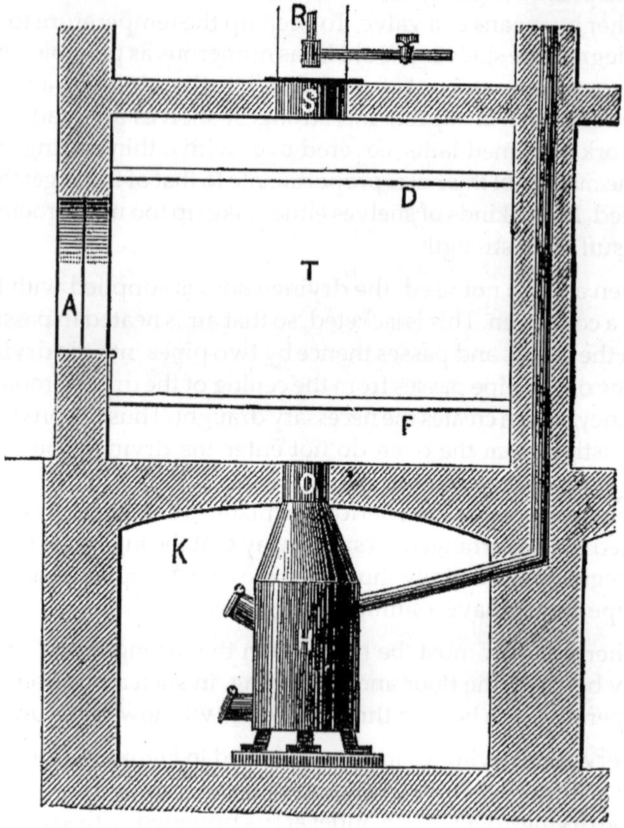

Figure 15

when they have lost from 80 to 90 per cent of their weight. In the press the dried vegetables are piled up in a mass, separated into layers of convenient thickness by iron plates. The thickness between the plates should be such that after the operation of the press the layers of vegetable are about half an inch thick. They are divided into equal portions, either during the pressing by edges projecting from the iron plates, which make the vegetable cake thinner along certain lines, so that it can be easily broken up into portions after leaving the press; or the press-cake is divided by stamps after it leaves the press. In either case the portions are supposed to furnish a meal for one person, and weigh about one ounce.

For transport the cakes are packed in boxes, for retail sale each is wrapped in paper bearing directions for use.

To use the portions, they are put in hot water. When the vegetable has expanded, it is cooked as if fresh, but takes rather longer than ordinary vegetables, as the cells have become more or less impervious.

The above process has been objected to, on the ground that the vegetables after a time have a haylike taste when cooked. Our experience shows that this trouble can only arise through an insufficient temperature being used in the drying-room, whereby vegetable-albumen is left uncoagulated. It is to changes in this uncoagulated albumen through the action of chemical ferments that the hay taste is due, and it is never noticeable if all the albumen has been coagulated.

Compressed vegetables must be kept dry, or they will very quickly become mouldy.

A very excellent plan for preserving vegetables is by cooking the vegetables with high-pressure steam, and then drying them with hot air. A steam chamber must be provided, through which first the steam and then the hot air is passed.

Chapter 30
Preservation of Vegetables by Appert's Method

For the more expensive sorts of vegetables, such as asparagus, green peas, etc., the Appert process is used exactly as described for meat. Glass vessels are generally used of the form shown in Figure 16. The vegetables are first cleaned and trimmed, and are then covered with water in the vessels, with or without a little salt. Sticks of asparagus, or whole beans, are stood on end. The vessels are now lightly corked and boiled in a bath of concentrated brine, in which they are stood upright as fully immersed as possible. The bath is heated very slowly, to avoid cracking the glass. It ought to take about two hours to bring the temperature to 100° C. The brine is then brought to the boil, whereupon the contents of the glasses will also boil. After they have been boiled for about ten minutes, the bath is allowed to cool to about 60° C., and the corks are driven tightly in. Fused paraffin is then poured over them; and when the bath is quite

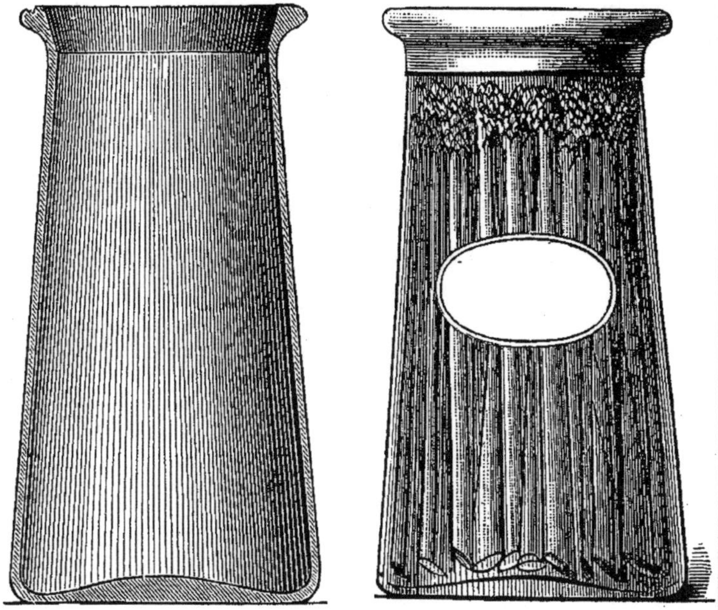

Figure 16

cold, the glasses are taken out. The vegetables will then keep for as long as the vessels are unopened, for all ferments in them have been destroyed, and the paraffined cork prevents any more from getting access to them. The paraffin on the cork should come flush with the edge of the jar, and should be tied over with vegetable parchment, to prevent it from cracking and flaking off. The top of the cork should be rough, that it may adhere better to the paraffin.

Mixed Pickles

This product, of English origin, has had a great success as an adjunct to meat. It is made from carefully chosen gherkins, green peas, young bean-pods; young onions, young maize-corns about 2 to 2½ inches long, and slices of carrot, together with pepper and other spices, preserved in not too strong salted vinegar. If the vinegar is too strong, the vegetables will shrivel up, from the abstraction of water from them by the acetic acid. The constitution of the mixture prevents the use of metal cans, which the vinegar would attack, and necessitates the employment of glass or earthenware.

The pickles are usually made by the Appert process, but as it is not necessary to cook the vegetables, an exposure to a temperature of from 80° to 90° for two or three hours, which will sterilise them, is enough. The taste is piquant, but not too sharp, and the pickles are excellent on board ship for preventing scurvy.

Chapter 31

The Preservation of Fruit

Fruits are preserved in very different ways. They may be dried whole or in pieces. They may be preserved in vinegar, syrup, alcohol, or glycerine, or by simple storage, according to certain definite rules. This last method will not, however, preserve fruit for more than a few months. Figs, peaches, and apricots can hardly be kept fresh for more than two or three weeks. The only fruits that can be stored for lengthened periods are those comparatively poor in water and having a strong protecting skin, *e.g.* apples and pears.

For preserving fruit on a large scale there are two processes of very great importance: storage and drying. The first is an extremely profitable business in or near large towns. The second is to be preferred in agricultural districts, where the fresh fruit is of small value. The fruit can then be sold for consumption elsewhere. Neither process is so easy as would at first appear. Even dried fruit is expected to retain its taste, colour, and aroma to a great extent. The full retention of the characters of the fruit is possible with stored fruit only. Hence the storage method of preservation is always to be adopted whenever possible.

Chapter 32

Preservation of Fruit by Storage

The first essential is that the fruit to be preserved must be in perfect condition. Every fruit must be carefully inspected, and the least wound or sign of unsoundness must at once cause its rejection. Unsound dark spots are certain to be already inhabited by mould, which will soon is store spread over the whole stock of fruit. Wounds also afford free access to spores.

Fruit must be stored according to the character of its skin. Only hard fruit, such as winter pears, may be laid direct on a hard shelf. If soft fruit is so laid, its own weight will in time break the skin. Cotton is often used to lay fruit on, but we have found that paper-cuttings are not only much cheaper but more elastic. The cuttings made by the bookbinder in trimming books are as good a material as can be used for the purpose. The paper-cuttings should, however, be sterilised before use, to prevent them from bringing ferments into contact with the fruit. This may be done by dipping them in boiling solution of alum, and then draining and drying them. Alum is thus left in the paper, and no ferment will ever be able to develop upon it.

The paper will also prevent any fruit-juice that, in spite of every precaution, may get squeezed out, from moulding. It is very desirable to paint the whole of the interior of the storeroom, shelves and all, with the alum solution. The alum should be applied hot, and a second coat when the first is dry should be given. The best flooring for the room is asphalt or cement. The room should be kept dark, and the windows should have double sashes. The temperature of the room should be a uniform and very low one, but always slightly above the freezing point of water. Too high a temperature favours decomposition, and the fruit is spoiled if it gets frozen, by the bursting of the tissues. The temperature should be kept, however, as near the freezing point as possible; 8° C. must be regarded as the highest point allowable under any circumstances. Too much warmth, besides favouring decomposition, partially dries and shrivels the fruit and spoils its appearance. The room is cooled with ice in the summer. Receptacles for the ice are provided against the walls near the ceiling. The walls of the storeroom should be thick and dry, and its exposure should be northerly. It should not open direct into the open air, but should have a vestibule between its door and the outer door. The space between the double sashes should be filled with sawdust, leaving a small space to admit light, and the windows should be provided with heavy shutters. Two apertures must be provided for ventilation, one near the floor the other near the ceiling. Both should be provided with dampers. Two thermometers must also be kept in the room, one near the floor the other near the ceiling.

Before the room is stocked, enough sulphur should be burnt in it to create just a slight smell, and that operation should be repeated once a fortnight, after putting in the fruit, so as to kill any incipient mouldiness that may have formed. The fruit must be carefully examined from time to time. Any mouldy specimens that may be found must be at once removed, and some sulphur burnt to destroy the spores floating in the air.

The fruits are simply placed on the paper-shavings in such a way that no two of them are in contact.

Fruit must never be stored too ripe, and it must be picked from the tree.

If the fruit can be wiped before being laid on the shelf, that should be carefully done with a clean flannel, but the process is inadmissible with downy fruits like peaches, or waxy ones like plums. The wiping is useful to remove spores and the eggs of insects.

Cherries, plums, and figs are best preserved with the stalks. With bunches of grapes, the cut end of the stalk is best dipped in shellac varnish, to prevent water from evaporating from it and causing the grapes to shrivel. The bunches should be hung up and not laid down.

When in the autumn the nights are cold but the days are still warm, the ventilators are opened at night to allow the warmer air in the room to be replaced by air from outside, and kept shut during the day. The ventilators should, however, never be opened in wet or misty weather, or the air in the room will become too damp. If in the winter there is fear of the fruit freezing, a large flower-pot filled with red-hot coals is put on the floor, and the thermometers are carefully watched.

In the manner and with the precautions above described, even such delicate fruits as peaches and figs may be kept without the least change for many months, and the profits of the undertaking, if carried out in or near a large town, are very great.

For preserving fruits by storage for very long periods, salicylic acid is most useful, especially for grapes, peaches, apricots, and other very susceptible kinds. A 1 per cent solution of the acid is made in pure 90 per cent alcohol, and the fruits are dipped in this for a moment, allowed to dry, and then stored at once. The evaporation of the alcohol leaves on the skin of the fruit a coating of salicylic acid, perceptible neither to the eye nor to the taste, but which is nevertheless an effectual barrier to the access of ferment spores. Many thin-skinned fruits, however, are turned dark brown by this treatment, which cannot therefore be applied to them.

If we perceive the skins of the stored fruit wrinkling, which happens most readily in thin-skinned plums, it is a sign that the air of the room has become too dry, and dishes of fresh water are set about on the floor.

There are many other ways of preserving fruit without drying it, but none give the excellent results above described. We shall therefore merely describe them briefly, and for the sake of completeness.

Apples, pears, and lemons can be kept well for long periods packed in charcoal powder or in slaked lime. The fruit and the powder are packed in a box in alternate layers, the bottom and top layer both being of the powder, and the spaces between the fruits being filled with it. If lime is used, it should first be sprinkled with a little dilute carbolic acid. Another way is to dip the fruit into fused paraffin for a second, and then to keep it hung up till the paraffin has set. The temperature of the paraffin is a matter of great importance, and should be between 62° and 66° C. Cooler it will not kill the spores, and hotter it will spoil the look of the fruit. It must, of course, be perfectly pure and odourless.

Chapter 33
The Preservation of Fruit by Drying

Fruits which are very rich in sugar, such as figs, dates, and grapes, can easily be air-dried to a state in which they will keep perfectly for very long periods. For example, figs in Southern Europe are sulphured and dried in the sun. When they have lost about two-fifths of their weight, they are gently flattened and packed in boxes with laurel leaves, or in casks, or are strung on threads. The best figs are packed in the first way. The inside of the fruit is then full of thick syrup, and sugar crystallises on the outside. The preservative action is of course due to the sugar, which will keep them for years.

Raisin-Manufacture

This important industry has not received the attention it deserves in Germany, but in Greece and Spain it is one of great magnitude. The famous Malaga raisins are got by allowing the bunches of grapes to dry in the air. They are dipped for an instant in boiling water to sterilise them, and then dried on straw in the sun. When the grapes have shrunk to a third or a half of their original volume (the richer they are in sugar the less drying they need), the best are packed in the original bunches, but the inferior raisins are plucked from the stalks before packing.

In Spain they dip the bunches into a boiling lye of wood ashes on which a little oil is floating. They are dipped and removed as quickly as possible, and the trace of oil which adheres to them gives a characteristic lustre.

In our Northern countries we can rarely dry grapes in the sun. A drying-room must be used, in which a temperature of 40° C. is enough. Raisin-manufacture can be strongly recommended to countries with an over-production of wine, such as Hungary and the Southern Steiermark.

Chapter 34
Drying Fruit by Artificial Heat

This can be done either with the fruit whole or after it has been cut up. The drying, too, may be gentle, or at high enough temperatures to cook the fruit as well as dry it.

Simple Drying with Warm Air

This process, which unfortunately is not yet much practised, gives a most praiseworthy product in the matters of durability and retention of the natural taste.

The fruit is dried on frames in a drying-room or in a cupboard, such as is shown in Figure 17, which is arranged to receive hot air from the jacket of a jacketed oven O. The hot air enters the drying chamber by the pipe R. The shelves are so arranged that the hot air has to pass over each one on its way to the outlet at S, where it joins the combustion gases from the stove, which make the draught. The current through the drying-room is regulated by a damper at S. As the fruit dries first on the bottom shelves, the shelves are slung by chains, so that when the bottom shelf is removed the whole set can

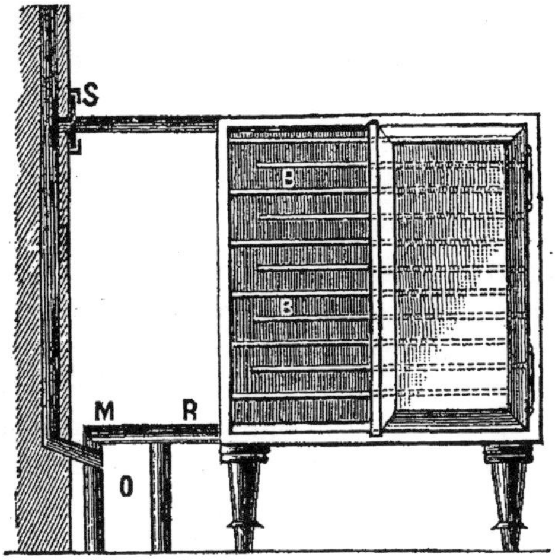

Figure 17

be pulled down, and the refilled shelf put on the top. Thus the work of removing and replacing shelves goes on continuously, and the drying is very rapid, with a small consumption of fuel.

Fine fruits are usually peeled and cut up before drying. This is done with apples and pears, for example, the core being first removed with a hollow punch. No steel must, however, be used for cutting or coring the fruit, as the traces of iron which dissolve give the fruit a black appearance after drying. The thermometer of the drying-room must not rise above 50° C. The temperature should be raised slowly at first, with the damper nearly closed. The steam coming from the fruit then warms them all equally. If the damper is then opened wide this steam escapes, and the hot air, which takes its place rapidly, brings the fruit to the proper point. The process is finished when the percentage of water in the fruit is down to about 12 per cent; but fruit which is dried without peeling, *e.g.* plums, pears, and apples, can have still more water left in them.

If care is not taken to heat the fruit gradually at first, the sudden production of steam may burst the cells, and cause the juice to extravasate. If plums are to be put upon the market without stones, they are kept first at a temperature between 30° and 35° C., until they have completely shrivelled. If then the plum is slowly pressed at one end, the stone will issue from the opposite end, and on further drying the aperture which it made in coming out will close completely.

If plums or peaches are to be dried without their skins, they are plunged for a few seconds in boiling water. The skin can then be easily removed by the fingers.

When the fruit leaves the drying chamber, it is cooled as quickly as may be, as experience has shown that they then retain a good lustre; while slowly cooled fruit shrivels and has an unattractive appearance. The best means of securing this object is to plunge the still hot fruit into a not too concentrated solution of sugar. This not only cools it rapidly, but gives it an appearance as if it had been varnished, by the formation, when the fruit has dried, of a thin external coat of sugar.

Chapter 35

Roasting Fruit

The foregoing method of drying fruit, although it is the only one to be recommended, is only scantily practised. In most places people are not content with driving off just so much water as is necessary for the preservation of the fruit, but actually roast it to hard shrivelled masses. Smyrna plums, for example, are particularly fine, but we rarely get them in a state which creates any suspicion of what they are in a fresh state. They come upon our market as hard black masses, which are scarcely edible until boiled. When this is done, they impart a bitter taste and a dark brown colour to the water. The sugar of the fruit has been caramelised by the high temperature to which the fruit has been subjected, and the caramel imparts its characteristic burnt and bitter taste. This completely conceals whatever may be left of the original taste of the fruit. The same taste is often noticeable in pears, which are then generally so hard that they require hours of boiling to make them eatable.

The roasting process is often carried out in an ordinary baker's oven, the fruit being treated exactly as if it were bread. In other places a special room is used. In this the fruit is exposed on shelves in trays of wood (or, better, of iron, as metal has greater conducting power than wood). The floor of the room is of iron plates, and the flues of the heating apparatus run just under it. The floor is made so hot that any fruit placed on it would be actually burnt, and the hot air rising from it circulates among the trays of fruit. There are openings in the ceiling for the escape of the steam from the fruit.

In such a room uniform heating is impossible, as the lower shelves must get much more heat than the upper ones, although attempts are often made to equalise matters by placing the largest fruits on the bottom shelves, and the small fruits and the pieces of those which have been cut up on the higher shelves.

The smell from such a room is perceptible at a considerable distance, and this is never the case with a proper drying-room.

Chapter 36

The Preservation of Fruit with Sugar

Fruits can be preserved in several ways by means of sugar. They may be packed in finely powdered sugar or candied, *i.e.* invested with a sugar crust. Another way is to keep the fruit in syrup strong enough to prevent the development of ferments.

The method of packing in powdered sugar is a little-known method well worthy of much more attention. The fruit is interstratified with the sugar, taking care that both the top and bottom layer is of sugar, and that sugar separates each fruit from all the rest in the same layer. In the use of this method the presence of a few damaged fruits does no harm, for the juice that oozes out makes a concentrated syrup with the sugar that cannot ferment.

Coating Fruits with Sugar

This process, although simple in the main, requires a good deal of skill with very juicy fruits to avoid injuring them.

For comparatively dry fruits, such as apples, pears, and orange or lemon peel, whole or in pieces, we proceed as follows: We take a weight of sugar equal to that of the fruit and heat it in a shallow dish on a water-bath to about 80° C. We then add a little water to the sugar and stir, so as gradually to bring it into solution. It is essential, by long and diligent stirring, to get as concentrated a syrup as possible. Into this the fruits are dipped separately, drained a little, and then laid on glass or other very smooth shelves. The hot syrup kills all the ferments and covers the fruit with a protective coating. Only sufficient sugar for immediate use should be heated, as prolonged heating converts the sugar into the uncrystallisable form. This is hygroscopic and makes the fruit sticky, so that when packed it forms huge lumps, which are hard to divide without breaking the fruit. With very juicy fruits, such as peaches and plums, the process should be as follows: The fruit is dipped in concentrated syrup at a temperature not exceeding 50° C., and is heated very slowly in it to 80°C. The fruit is then removed and dried in a current of warm air. The reason of this variation of the process is that if the juicy fruit were dipped into syrup at 80°C. the great and sudden change of temperature would burst the skin and spoil the fruit. The drying in warm air gives the lustre which properly sugared fruit should have.

Preservation of Fruit in Syrup

To preserve fruit in syrup, perfect fruits are peeled and cored when desirable. Plums must always have the stone removed. Peaches and apricots should be cut in halves and stoned. Wide-mouthed glass vessels are generally used, and these should be first scalded out. The fruit is put in, and the glasses are then stood in water of about 40° to 60° C. Concentrated syrup of the same temperature is then poured in, taking care to allow no sugar to drip on the mouth of the vessel. Damp parchment paper is then stretched over the mouth, and the water outside is brought to the boil. The glasses are left in the boiling water from twenty to eighty minutes, according to their size, so that they may be heated through and all ferments in them killed. The glasses are then removed and tied down while still hot. Very delicate and aromatic fruits, such as strawberries and raspberries, should always be put into small glasses, because these require only a short heating, which does not dissipate much of the aroma.

We wish to remark specially that although many people consider boiling the fruit in the syrup an essential condition of successful preservation, such boiling is not only absolutely unnecsssary, but is in fact injurious, as the temperature of the boiling syrup is very high and shrivels the fruit, quite spoiling its appearance. Moreover, the skins become as tough as leather, and all aroma is completely driven away.

Eastern nations, such as the Indians, the Javanese, and the Japanese, appear to understand the art of preserving fruit perfectly. We have had repeated opportunities in England of tasting their fruits preserved in syrup. Most of them were of a very spicy nature,–too much so, in fact, to be liked by the majority of Europeans. The pine-apples and ginger preserved in the East are a striking proof of skill in fruit-preserving. The pine-apples retain their form and colour and their aroma and taste to perfection. The ginger had kept its powerful burning aromatic taste in the fullest degree. These preserves come to Europe in earthenware pots, usually painted blue, and packed in rush-baskets.

Chapter 37

Boiled Preserved Fruit

The methods just described of preserving fruit in syrup are combinations of the Appert process with the use of an antiseptic substance. The Appert process can, however, be used alone. In this case plain water can be used, although for the sake of the flavour, weak syrup is better, and the fruit is thoroughly cooked before the tin is soldered up. It is unnecessary that the fruit should be entirely immersed, as the immersed part gets thoroughly cooked by the steam developed.

Chapter 38

The Preservation of Fruit in Spirit, Acetic Acid, or Glycerine

Spirit, acetic acid, and glycerine are all water-subtracting substances, which can be used for the preservation of fruit. Acetic acid being sour is more used for preserving vegetables than fruit. When it is employed, the fruit is heated with it in glasses to the boiling point of water, and then immediately fastened down. Cucumbers are carefully washed, rolled while still wet in salt, and then covered with boiling vinegar in stoneware pots. The pot is then securely covered with paraffined paper. The cucumbers will then be perfectly preserved, with their taste and colour unchanged.

The preservation of fruit in spirit is a very commendable process, although it is seldom properly executed. The usual fault is to use the spirit much too strong. Such spirit keeps the fruit perfectly, it is true, but in time gives it a toughness which defies all human mastication.

Besides, the spirit extracts the colour, flavour, and aroma of the fruit completely, leaving nothing but a mass of tasteless cellulose. This property of concentrated spirit makes it very suitable for preparing fruit-essences and liqueurs, but makes it very unsuitable for preserving the fruit itself. For this purpose even ordinary brandy containing from 22 to 25 per cent of absolute alcohol is quite strong enough to prevent fermentation. This is the strength therefore that should be used in fruit-preserving.

The alcohol should, however, always be bought strong, of 80 per cent strength at least, and diluted with water. The reason of this is that it must be free from fusel oil, and the only alcohols on the market that are free from it are the highest strengths. The presence of fusel oil, with its foul smell and taste, is fatal to the flavour of the fruit. Experience has shown that it is quite impossible to make a good fruit-preserve or liqueur with potato spirit. It puts the finest fruit on a level with the very commonest kinds.

In some cases, however, the taste of consumers has become so prejudiced that it is actually necessary to use spirit containing fusel oil. It is well known that nuts are preferred preserved in rum, which owes its special flavour to a particular sort of fusel oil. The same remark applies to the preservation of peaches in cherry brandy, a liquid which forms the basis of maraschino. These two fruits are in Germany practically the only ones ever preserved in spirit, although the preserves so obtained are of excellent quality. In France, on the other hand, it is very common to preserve fruits in brandy.

Even when the spirit is used of the proper strength, a great deal of flavour passes in time out of the fruit into the spirit, so that the spirit is consumed together with the fruit. The extraction is chiefly due to osmosis, resulting from the difference between the density of the spirit and that of the juice of the fruit. To diminish it, it is advisable to add sugar to the alcohol. The following solution preserves fruit admirably:

Sugar .... 15 lb.

80 per cent spirit .... 10 lb.

Water .... 75 lb.

Glycerine is another most excellent preservative for fruit. It must be quite free from colour or smell, and must be properly diluted like spirit. The best proportions are one gallon of concentrated glycerine to four or five gallons of water. Stronger glycerine abstracts too much water from the fruit, and shrivels and toughens it. Fruit preserved in glycerine lasts as long as that preserved in alcohol, and tastes as if it had been preserved in syrup.

Chapter 39

Preservation of Fruit Without Boiling

We have succeeded in preserving fruit perfectly without any heating whatever. The results have been so good, the fruit tasting after very prolonged periods as if it had been gathered only a few hours before, that we here publish it. It depends on the antiseptic qualities of salicylic acid, which is used in concentrated solution in water. The acid is put into an enamelled iron vessel with 200 times its weight of water, and is then heated with constant stirring. The moment, however, the water begins to boil, the pot is removed from the fire and placed where it will not be disturbed. The solution is decanted from the sediment when quite cold, and is concentrated. The sediment, which consists of acid which dissolved in the hot water but separated out again on cooling, is preserved for a fresh solution. The fruit is simply preserved in the solution in jars or glasses tied over with vegetable parchment.

When the fruit is eaten the taste of the salicylic acid is hardly perceived even by the most delicate palate.

To prevent the loss of flavour, which takes place in time, just as when fruit is preserved in dilute alcohol, the same remedy is adopted as in that case. Sugar is dissolved in the salicylic acid in quantities according to taste. If very much sugar is used, it should not be put into hot solution of salicylic acid, or it will hinder the settling down of the acid thrown out on cooling, and the syrup will be made turbid by solid floating particles. In this case the sugar must be dissolved in the cold acid solution. For weak syrups it is best to use the hot solution, which dissolves the sugar more quickly.

Care must be taken not to infringe the law in using this process. In countries where the use of salicylic acid is forbidden, fruit must not be preserved for sale by means of it.

The Preparation of Preserved Fruit-Juices

As is well known, it is customary in the case of certain aromatic fruits to preserve the juice only. This juice is then either consumed as such or used for making ratafia and other fruit beverages, or ices and similar confectionery. It goes without saying that the preservation of the aromatic taste is a matter of the first importance. The chief juices preserved are those of the pine-apple, raspberry, and strawberry, but certain kinds of apples and pears also give excellent results.

The first thing to be done is to pick the fruit with the greatest care and to reject all green berries and damaged fruits. Raspberries and strawberries are then slightly bruised, and apples or pine-apples crushed to a coarse paste. The fruit is then interstratified in equal layers with sugar, the top and bottom layer being each of sugar. This operation is carried out in a large glass flask fitted with a cork perforated with two holes. Through one of the holes a glass tube passes nearly to the bottom of the flask.

The flask is now placed in a room where the temperature does not exceed 10° C. until all appearance of sugar has gone. This takes a day or two, and is helped by frequent shaking of the flask. When no more sugar can be seen, the flask is inverted over a hair-sieve until no more syrup drops out from it. The residue in the flask is mixed with its own bulk of water and strongly pressed. The resulting liquid is saved for a further stage of the operation.

The liquid which has run through the sieve, is poured into an enamelled pot surrounded by nearly boiling water, which is then quickly boiled up and kept boiling till the juice has reached the same temperature, as shown by a thermometer in it. The juice is stirred all the time. When the heating is over, the hot juice is filtered without delay into bottles through paper. The coagulated albumen of the juice remains on the filters, and the juice in the bottles is perfectly clear and will keep its taste and aroma unimpaired.

It is a better plan, although it requires more care, to heat the juice over an open fire. This not only saves time by bringing the juice to the necessary temperature more quickly, but at the same time, when the heating is more prolonged, there is less loss of aroma by volatilisation. The stirring must, however, be thorough and unremitting, or the juice will burn, and the pot must be taken from the fire the instant a temperature of 100° C. is reached. Nothing is gained by using a higher temperature than 100°C. The quality of the product suffers, on the other hand.

For making ices these fruit-juices are left as prepared. For beverages, however, they are too sweet for most tastes, and they are diluted before filtering with the cooled solution of salicylic acid above described.

Aromatic apples and quinces must not be peeled before being prepared, as most of the aroma is in the peel.

If it is desired to give a fruit-juice a flavouring with some other fruit, a little of the essential oil of the latter should be rubbed up with sugar, which is then dissolved in the first juice.

Chapter 40

Jam-Manufacture

Jam generally means a fruit-pulp preserved with sugar. Jams are much used by confectioners, and their preparation answers quite well with second-rate fruit, as there is no appearance to keep up.

When a fruit-juice is heated to the boil very gradually, we find that it undergoes a particular change, which is specially well marked with raspberry juice. The liquid gradually thickens, and may do so to such an extent as to gelatinise on cooling.

The cause of this phenomenon is the presence in the juice of a substance called pectin, which is dissolved in the fresh juice, but which on long heating becomes converted into pectic acid, which has the property of gelatinising on cooling, so that juices containing much of it form a perfect jelly when afterwards allowed to cool.

The change from pectin to pectic acid is a species of fermentation caused by a chemical ferment named pectose. This, like most chemical ferments, requires a high temperature to bring it into action. Hence if fruit-juice is wanted the crushed fruit must be kept as cool as possible, and the heating of the juice must be got over quickly, so as not to allow time for the formation of much pectic acid. When gelatinisation has taken place, filtration is impossible, and the product must be utilised as a jam or a fruit jelly.

To make jams the fruit is bruised or grated. Soft fruits, such as strawberries, raspberries, mulberries, etc., are best ground in a thick enamelled pot with a wooden pestle. Apples, quinces, and firm-fleshed fruit generally, are rubbed up with a grater. A good grating machine for work on a large scale may be made by mounting a horizontal roller, as shown in Figure 18. This roller has a surface like a rasp. Above it is a hopper, in which the fruit is placed, and pressed down upon the rotating grater by means of a weighted board.

We may here allude to the use of copper or brass utensils in confectionery-making. Such articles are always tinned, on account of the risk of copper or brass imparting poisonous properties to the confectionery. Such apparatus is very expensive, and must be carefully watched to detect any injury to the coating of tin. The presence of the least scratch laying bare the brass or copper necessitates the immediate retinning of the utensil, as the vegetable acids in fruit dissolve copper or brass with great rapidity, forming metallic compounds, which are highly poisonous even in very small doses. Any manufacturer using imperfectly tinned copper or brass implements, or having fruit-preparations in stock which contain copper, should be liable to the severest penalties. Again, inasmuch as jams and jellies can only be made during the fresh-fruit season of the year, there is then a great rush, and it is impossible to spare any utensils that require retinning. On these grounds we cannot too

Figure 18

urgently recommend the entire banishment of all copper and brass implements and receptacles from fruit factories, and their replacement by others made of harmless materials. Nothing is better for receptacles of all kinds than iron. This need not even be enamelled inside, so long as it is kept clean, but enamel does no harm so long as it is free from lead. Iron does equally well for tools, such as ladles, spatulas, etc. Even hard wood answers quite well for these. Brass sieves, too, should never be used, but such as are made of horse hair or iron wire. Everything used must be kept scrupulously clean.

The amount of sugar required in jam-making depends on the fruit. For fruits very rich in sugar–such as mulberries, strawberries, and raspberries–15 to 20 lb. of sugar is enough for 100 lb. of fruit. But for very sour fruit, such as gooseberries, much more is necessary. It is quite unnecessary to use the best sugar. This must be taken for fruit-juices, but for jams ordinary castor is quite good enough. Loaf should not be bought, as the labour of grinding is thereby incurred. The sugar is mixed with the fruit pulp, which has been sieved either in the dry state or in a paste with a little hot water. In any case it must be thoroughly mixed in. The jam is next kept at a temperature of from 30° to 40° C. for a long time in an iron pan, till it has thickened from the formation of pectic acid. If this heating is done over an open fire, the mass must be stirred without an instant's cessation the whole time the pan is being heated, or it is certain to burn, an accident to which its syrupy nature and bad conductivity for heat make it peculiarly liable. The very least occurrence of this mishap darkens the jam and spoils its taste. A steam jacket is far preferable to a naked fire, and prevents all fear of burning. Such a steam jacketed pan is illustrated in Figure 19. The pan is best swung on hollow trunnions, through which the steam passes. The fact that the steam can be instantly turned off, not only minimises the risk of burning, but secures a great economy of heat.

When the jam has thickened, its temperature is raised to 100° C. to kill its ferments. It is then poured hot into the jars in which it is to be sold, and these are at once covered down. Glass vessels should be heated to 40° to 50° C. before they are filled. This can be done by standing them on a grating in a current of hot air.

To make matters quite sure, the pots may be heated in boiling water after they are filled and tied down.

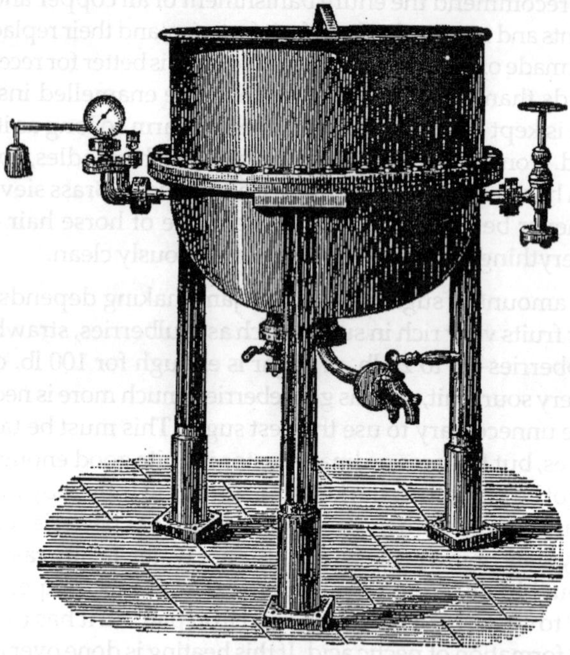

Figure 19

When a jam has been kept for a very long time, its upper part hardens to a thick crust by gradual evaporation. This can be prevented by making the cover impervious to water vapour with paraffin or with a quickly drying varnish.

Properly prepared jams have a uniform transparent texture, the same colour as the juice of the fruit and a thickness proportionate to the amount of sugar present. Some are difficult to get thick enough, currant jam for example. To remedy this, some raspberry juice is added before the heating. This juice is very rich in pectose, and rapidly converts the pectin present into pectic acid.

Chapter 41

The Manufacture of Fruit Jellies

Fruit jellies differ from jams simply in keeping the shape of a mould after they are removed from it, and forming a coherent trembling mass like a gelatine jelly.

The manufacture consists in breaking up the fruit as described for jam. The pulp is then packed in linen bags, which are subjected to the power of a screw or hydraulic press. The pressure must be applied gradually, or the strongest bags will burst and the juice squirt about and be wasted. The liquid pressed out is mixed with a great quantity of sugar, in some cases with as much as its own weight. Some juices need so much sugar to thicken them that the taste of the fruit is almost entirely concealed. This is the case, for example, with strawberries, and in this and all other similar cases the device of adding raspberry juice is adopted to avoid spoiling the taste with too much sugar. Of course no more must be added than is necessary, for the raspberry flavour must be kept as far as possible in the background. Ten per cent of raspberries, reckoned on the weight of the other fruit, is enough even for the thinnest juices.

The slow heating, to give the pectose time to act, is essential, and is best done on a water-bath. The heating is continued until a few drops, allowed to drip from a spatula on to a cold stone, gelatinise quickly. If the mass will not gelatinise, more sugar must be added, stirring it in a little at a time.

All temptation to hurry matters by using more heat must be absolutely resisted, for fear of burning the mass. The least suspicion of this ruins the whole beyond repair, by forming caramel. The colour of this is quite sufficient to darken the jelly and make it opaque.

The jelly is poured hot either into moulds or into shallow pans. In the latter case it is further cut up with a wire after it has set. The pans or moulds should be warmed before the jelly is poured in, so that the jelly may set slowly. The appearance and transparency are then much better than if the jelly sets quickly.

Fruit jellies are very hygroscopic, and hence soon absorb enough water from the air to become sticky. Hence they must be put in boxes as soon as they are taken from the moulds, and separated from one another by sheets of paper. The finest qualities are wrapped in tinfoil, each piece separately.

Chapter 42

The Making of Gelatine Jellies

Independently of the trouble it involves, the manufacture of jellies out of purely vegetable matter is a somewhat costly process. To remedy this, gelatine is often added to them, whereby a notable saving in sugar is effected. Only the very purest gelatine must be used, however, as any taste or smell of glue would of course make the jelly utterly unsaleable. Pure gelatine being rather dear, it is best to prepare it or to obtain it by purifying ordinary glue. To do this we take the best white gold-size, and place it in a mixture of ten volumes of water and one of vinegar. Here the glue is left for an hour. The liquid is then changed, and again every hour till the glue has swollen as much as it can, and is a nearly colourless and elastic mass. The glue thus purified may be dissolved at once, or dried in warm air for future use. It will be found to be quite tasteless and so nearly colourless as not to interfere with the transparency of the jellies. It is somewhat more troublesome to prepare gelatine from calves' feet, but still it is cheaper than buying it. All that needs to be done is to give the chopped-up feet a prolonged boiling in water. The best method is to put the chopped feet, free from bone, into a clean linen bag, which is hung in the boiling water. The gelatine solution then sinks to the bottom as it is formed, and the action proceeds very rapidly. The use of the bag also obviates the necessity of filtering the solution. When finished, the solution is poured into flat pans to gelatinise. If we make gelatine habitually, it is very convenient to have a digester, in which the process, under high pressure, is very rapid indeed. The solution from the digester is filtered hot through linen and allowed to gelatinise.

The gelatine is used for fruit jellies as follows: The fruit-juice sweetened with sugar is heated slowly, to form as much pectic acid as possible, and then mixed with the gelatine previously coarsely powdered (it is as brittle as glass when dry). The gelatine is added a little at a time till a sample tested as above directed shows a sufficient gelatinisation.

Another method is to add the sugar to the hot gelatine solution and then to put in the fruit-juice until the mass has the proper taste. Care must be taken to have neither too little sugar nor too little fruit-juice, or the taste of the gelatine will be plainly perceptible.

In the case of these gelatine fruit jellies there is not enough sugar to make the jellies keep, at least in a damp atmosphere. To remedy this the jelly is placed on a piece of iron wire gauze, and rapidly dipped in a concentrated syrup which is on the point of crystallising. This covers the jelly with a coating of pure sugar. This not only keeps out ferment spores, but makes the jelly firmer and easier to store and pack.

It is very common to dye these jellies to correspond with the colour of the fruit. The dye must be harmless and soluble in water, and must always be added to the fruit-juice before the latter is heated. For yellow or brown the best dye is caramel, but it must be specially made, so as to be free from all bitter taste. For red cochineal is used, or the juice of very dark cherries. The cherry-juice has always a violet shade, which never gives a good pure red when diluted. With cochineal or kermes, any colour from the most delicate pink to the darkest scarlet can be obtained.

Just as the jellies can be artificially coloured, so an artificial aroma can be imparted to them. This can be done with the fruit essences of commerce, which go an extremely long way, and must therefore be used in very small quantities or the use of them will be at once detected.

Agar-agar, which is sold in the form of a white leafy mass, is made from East Indian seaweed, and on long boiling with water gives a solution which on cooling forms a colourless and tasteless jelly. The gelatinising power of agar-agar is eight times as great as that of the finest gelatine. This property, which enables it to be used in much smaller proportions than gelatine, together with its absolute want of taste or colour, makes agar-agar highly suitable for the preparation of fruit jellies, and, in fact, the best of them are now made with agar-agar exclusively.

Chapter 43
The Manufacture of Sulzen

When a jelly is made, not from the whole pulp of the fruit, but from the juice alone, rapidly heated to clarify it by coagulating its albumen, it is called (in Germany) a *Sulze* (plural, *Sulzen*).

As the heating causes the juice to lose its gelatinising power, gelatine or agar-agar must always be used in this manufacture. The jelly properly prepared has a glassy appearance, and is either quite transparent or nearly so.

The preparation is a very simple matter. As much gelatine or agar-agar as is wanted is melted over the water-bath. It is too risky to melt it over an open flame. It almost invariably gets burnt, whatever care is taken. The strongly heated sugared fruit-juice is then poured into it, the mass is dyed if required, and the whole is poured into a warm mould to set slowly. The slower it sets the clearer the result. If, however, the jelly has not set sufficiently in ten or twelve hours, it should be put in a cold cellar or, better still, on ice. After that the jelly will last a long time without breaking down, even in a warm room.

If the jellies have to be stocked, they must be made by stirring enough powdered gelatine into the clear hot fruit-juice, to make it set hard and glassy on quick cooling. When still hot, the mass is poured into warm moulds, and as soon as the contents have set, they are wrapped in paper or, better, in tinfoil. If they contain very little water the jelly will keep for months. These hard jellies may also be made by using a very concentrated solution of agar-agar in small quantities.

Chapter 44

The Preservation of Fermented Beverages

Wine and beer are very prone to go sour. They can be preserved by heating them to the ferment-killing temperature, which for them is from 60° to 65° C. Red wines, which are not altered by the heating, are best subjected to it in bottle. The bottles are immersed in water, which is then very gradually brought to a temperature of from 70° to 80° C., and then allowed to cool again gradually. White wine, which if so treated throws out coagulated albumen a day or two afterwards, must be poured out before heating it. This heating is best done by making the wine pass through a tin worm immersed in boiling water, and at such a rate that the wine as it comes out has a temperature of about 65° C. The wine is then cooled by passing through another tin worm immersed in cold water, and runs into a cask, where it stays till all the coagulated albumen has settled to the bottom. It is then rebottled.

Beer will not stand such a temperature as 60° C. If, however, bottled beer is kept for an hour or an hour and a half at from 45° to 48° C., its qualities are not impaired, while the ferments, although not killed, are so weakened that the beer will keep for a year or eighteen months perfectly well.

The above process for wine was discovered by Pasteur, and is known as pasteurising. Many other liquids, such as fruit-wine, vinegar, and milk, can be preserved in the same way. Pasteurised milk will keep in a closed bottle for at least a week in the very hottest summer weather.

Part II
The Manufacture of Sweetmeats

Chapter 45
Introduction

In the narrow sense, the word "candies" means eatables covered with crystallised sugar. In its wider sense it includes all confectionery products except cakes and tarts. We distinguish, therefore, candied fruit, caramels, bonbons, dragées, pralines, rocks, etc.

While in earliest times the trades of the confectioner and of the fruit-preserver–the French word *confiseur* means fruit-preserver–were united, as they are still in small towns, they are now entirely separated when practised on a large scale. There are factories devoted exclusively to the preservation of fruit, and others in which candies alone, in the narrow sense, are made. The confectioner and the cake-maker find their account in dealing with dragées only, for the erection of a dragée plant on a large scale is an expensive matter. Machinery not only provides quicker and cheaper results than hand labour, but gives a much more uniform product than even the most skilled workman.

If we use the process described in chapter 36, we obtain fruit with a thin glassy sugar-coating like a varnish, which prevents evaporation, and also prevents the entrance of spores. The process must not, however, be confounded with candying. In that we get a far thicker sugar crust. The fruit must look as if covered with ice, and not have the smooth shining appearance of fruit preserved by the method just alluded to.

Chapter 46
The Manufacture of Candied Fruit

Candied fruit is fruit covered with a thick crust of sugar. The sugar is not always used pure, but often in a partially caramelised state, or partly converted into uncrystallisable sugar. As the appearance of the candy depends greatly on the sugar, it will be advisable to begin with the methods of preparing the sugar.

When sugar is heated, it melts at a comparatively low temperature to a clear liquid, which forms a mass like glass on cooling. This mass gradually becomes opaque on keeping, by gradually becoming traversed by minute cracks as a result of the formation of a vast number of very small crystals.

It requires, however, great precaution to melt cane-sugar without changing it. If the sugar is heated in the least above the fusion point, it becomes yellow from the formation of a trace of caramel, a substance of very great colouring power. Many manufacturers, however, consider it necessary to clarify the sugar before using it, or else to melt it. The process is, however, quite unnecessary with pure sugar.

Although pure sugar is somewhat dear, it is always best to use it for candying, as inferior sugars are never pure even after clarifying, and detract greatly from the flavour of the fruit.

Clarifying

This process is carried out either with white of egg or with animal-charcoal. Blood has been proposed as a substitute for white of egg, and blood-charcoal for ordinary bone-charcoal. It is necessary, however, to protest against the use of these bodies. Blood contains not only the albumen to which it owes its clarifying properties, but a number of salts which remain in the clarified sugar, and is, besides, often difficult to get in a fresh state. The use of blood in a state of incipient putridity would give the sugar a taste and smell which would absolutely prevent any use being made of it. Blood-charcoal, which is got by heating blood in closed vessels, does very well, but as it is dearer than bone-charcoal, it is difficult to see any reason for using it.

We should therefore always clarify sugar with egg-albumen or with bone-charcoal, and this should be done whenever the sugar forms a yellow solution with water, or has any unpleasant smell or taste.

For the highest class of candied fruits, picked fruit and perfectly pure sugar must be used. In this case, the clarification of the sugar is not only a work of supererogation, but is actually injurious, however carefully it may be done.

Clarification with Egg-Albumen

The sugar is placed in a clean iron pan, in which the water and egg-albumen have been previously placed. The usual quantities are about 27 quarts of water and the whites of 10 eggs for every 2 cwt. of sugar. The albumen is beaten up with a little of the water to a froth, and then mixed with the rest of the water in the pan. The sugar is next put in. The pan is slung over a fire in such a way that it can be instantly removed if necessary, and so that its sides are heated as well as its bottom.

Before heating the pan, its contents are thoroughly mixed with a slice. The stirring must be kept up without any interruption throughout the heating to prevent the sugar sticking to the pan and getting burnt. Until all the sugar is dissolved, the temperature of the contents of the pan should not exceed 50° C. Then, however, the pan is heated as quickly as possible to 70°C. The albumen then coagulates, and gives the liquid a milky appearance. The flakes of albumen enclose all the solid impurities in the sugar and the colouring matter.

The moment the coagulation is finished, the temperature is brought down again to 50°C. as quickly as possible. The albumen rises to the top as a dirty white scum, together of course with the impurities it has entangled. This is carefully and thoroughly removed, usually with a drainer. A better plan, however, is to use an iron ring fixed to a handle and covered with coarse gauze. The ring should be about six inches in diameter. The scum is kept apart in a special vessel, and when there is a sufficient accumulation of it, it is treated to recover the sugar from it, which is then used for second-rate goods.

The above rules for heating during this process cannot be too strictly observed, and it must be remembered that every degree of temperature above that necessary to coagulate the albumen at the particular point indicated, or above the temperature required to keep the mass liquid at all the other stages, is injurious. Any excess, especially if the sugar is boiled, produces a brown colour. It is, in fact, an excellent plan to replace the open fire by a water-bath. It is true that in this case rather more fuel is required, but all burning of the sugar is rendered impossible, as its temperature can never reach 100° C.

As soon as the syrup is free from scum, it is either used at once for candying or is poured into shallow vessels to set.

Clarification with Bone-Charcoal

This is done by mixing the sugar with water in the pan, and then adding finely powdered bone-charcoal. To every 2 cwt. of sugar we take 27 quarts of water and 11 lb. of the charcoal. This is made into a paste with its own weight of the water before being added. It is then poured into the rest of the ingredients in a thin stream, the temperature of the pan being kept between 50° and 60° C. the while, and with constant stirring. About half an hour after all the charcoal is in, the mass, still at the same temperature, is filtered through a felt pocket hung up by four strings. A second filtration through another bag may be necessary.

The scum is treated by mixing it with water, and filtering the solution of sugar from the coagulated albumen.

These clarifying processes have been made of almost entirely academic interest by the improvements in sugar-refining. These have put perfectly pure sugar, which only needs dissolving in clear water, within easy reach.

The sugar is used for candying in combination with water to the extent of about 30 per cent. In making this nearly concentrated syrup, the sugar is simply placed in the necessary amount of water and occasionally stirred till dissolved. If it is desired to accelerate the solution by heat, a temperature of 50° C. must never be exceeded. The syrup will keep indefinitely. It should of course be covered up to prevent dust from getting at it. Even dust-free syrups, if they are not strong enough to crystallise, get clearer on standing.

Chapter 47

The Manufacture of Boiled Sugar and Caramel

When we heat pure sugar, or sugar melted with water, it begins to decompose at rather a low temperature. The sugar turns to a yellow colour, which gradually gets deeper to a reddish brown, becoming with further heating a dark brown. The mass then begins to blister and froth up and emits empyreumatic vapours, and finally becomes quite black.

At a temperature a little above 200° C. nothing remains but a very porous form of charcoal.

If the heating has been so managed that the colour is a dark brown, and the sugar forms a glassy mass on cooling, the product is called caramel. At lower temperatures we have burnt-sugar merely, which is a mixture of caramel and unchanged sugar in proportions depending on the temperature used. Several such mixtures are used in candying, and there are certain empirical signs whereby we may know the condition of the sugar at any given point. As these signs are of great practical importance, we must describe them in some detail.

When the sugar drops from the stirring stick drawn out into threads, the degree is known as weak or strong thread as the case may be. Sugar which is not heated beyond this point, should be quite colourless and transparent on cooling. As more water evaporates and the temperature gets higher, a sample taken out with a ladle and poured back forms on the main mass spherical globules, which gradually mingle with the rest. At this stage a sample allowed to cool till it can be handled, will make an unbroken thread if a little of it is pinched between the thumb and forefinger, when the two are separated as far as possible. This point is known as pearl. The next stage is called blow. At this stage bubbles can be made in a little of the sugar in a skimming ladle, by blowing down the hollow handle of the implement. After a little more heating, little bubbles fly on blowing from the opening of the hollow handle into the bowl. This stage is called feather. When a sample poured on a cold stone sets to a hard and very brittle mass, the stage is known as weak or strong crack. By this time the sugar has a deep brown colour, and contains a large amount of caramel, but there is, however, still some unchanged sugar left.

Caramel

Caramel is the result of heating beyond the crack point. It has a dark brown, almost black, colour, is extremely soluble in water, and has no taste. If too high a temperature is used in making it, however, it acquires a very bitter taste, owing to the presence of a substance called assamar, which caramel should not contain. In making caramel the mass must be continually stirred, and the process should be carried out in a well-ventilated room, as the fumes produced act powerfully on the eyes.

The process of making caramel may be described as follows: Having put a little sugar into the pan, add a very small quantity of water to it, and heat carefully to fusion. When fusion is complete, add a little more sugar, and so on, till all the sugar to be treated is in, stirring persistently all the time. This method of procedure admits of the sugar being melted with a minimum of water, whereby fuel and time are both saved, for the whole of the water must be evaporated before any caramel can be formed. During the stirring the slice should be lifted out occasionally, so as to mix the upper and lower portions of the mass. In treating large quantities, two stirrers should relieve each other until the end. Then both must be at work, for vigorous stirring is essential, and numbers of samples have to be examined. The samples are poured in the form of strings on plates of tinned iron. These strings should show a dark reddish-brown colour by transmitted light when the process is finished. Thicker ones, say of the thickness of a lead pencil, must be quite opaque and look like black glass. The fracture must be smooth and flat. The taste is of importance. A sweetish gummy taste shows insufficient heating, while a bitter taste shows that the process has been overdone. The heating must then be at once suspended before it is too late. As before mentioned, caramel should have no taste.

Absence of taste is the great test, and is very difficult to secure working with large quantities at a time. In most cases the finished mass is slightly bitter. If the taste is only slight, it is of little moment, as the colouring power of caramel is so great that only very little of it has to be used, so that the bitter becomes very feeble indeed, and is usually effectually concealed.

As caramel is usually made in fairly large quantities, it is important to keep it in its soluble state. As soon as it is finished, it is cast hot into shallow pans. The brittle mass is broken up the instant it has set, and is then coarsely powdered and put into vessels while still warm, and the receptacles are immediately closed air-tight. If these precautions are neglected, the caramel absorbs water from the air and forms sticky masses, which dissolve with great difficulty.

Caramel is generally used in the form of solution, and the solution should always be kept in stock. A highly concentrated solution can be easily prepared by nearly filling a bottle with the coarsely powdered caramel, and then filling up with water. The solution formed is very permanent. Diluted solutions, on the other hand, mould very quickly, and should therefore only be made from the concentrated solution when required for immediate use.

Chapter 48
The Candying of Fruit

The process is very analogous to that for preparing sugar-candy. This is made by stretching threads in a very concentrated syrup, which is then covered over and left where it will not get shaken. The whole mass sets to a block of hard crystals, which is generally put on the market unbroken. In candying fruit, however, the formation of large crystals must be avoided. When a syrup is so concentrated at a high temperature that it deposits part of its sugar on cooling somewhat, a further cooling quickly causes the formation of numerous small crystals. This is the principle of fruit-candying. A sugar solution made at a certain temperature is poured over the fruit after cooling to a certain point, and after a time the fruit is removed. The sugar-boiling degree used varies with the fruit. It must be higher for watery fruits, such as melons and pine-apples, than for drier ones.

The candying is done in special iron vessels. As large batches as possible should be worked to save time, labour, and fuel. Very usual dimensions are 20 in. by 12 in. by 8 in. A frame covered with wire-netting is fitted parallel to the bottom of the box, and about mid-way in the depth of the box. At one corner a hole with a cork is provided, for running out the sugar syrup after the candying is finished. The fruits to be candied are put on the bottom of the box, but not too close together, as they are increased in size by the sugar crust. If two become stuck together, the appearance is spoiled in breaking them apart. The frame is next put in its place, and also covered with fruit, and the syrup is then poured in sufficient quantity to cover the top layer. In pouring in the syrup, care must be taken that the pieces of fruit are not moved and brought into contact with one another. When the syrup is in, the vessel is covered over and left for twenty-four hours for the crystals to form. The syrup is then run off, and the fruit, when it has drained, is dried in a drying-room. The process is rather troublesome, on account of the care necessary in placing the fruit. Small vessels, moreover, cool too rapidly for good crystallisation. In Figure 20 a vessel is shown which permits a large number of pieces to be candied perfectly with the greatest possible economy of space. As the transverse section shown indicates, the vessel is trough-shaped and about 6 ft. 8 in. long, and the depth and the width at the bottom are each about 16 in. The material is wood. At S the opening for emptying out the syrup and its stopper are shown. The steps running along the sides of the trough are about 3 in. high. At one end of the box is the vertical funnel R.

Figure 21 shows one of the wire-netting frames used in this trough. They are, of course, made of different sizes to fit the steps in the trough. The netting is of tinned iron wire, and the frame is

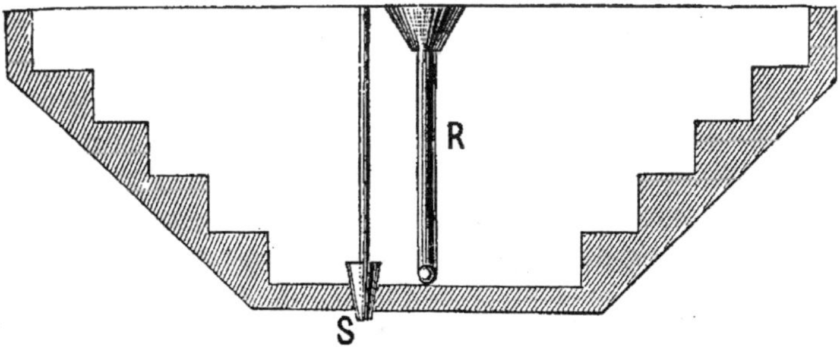

Figure 20

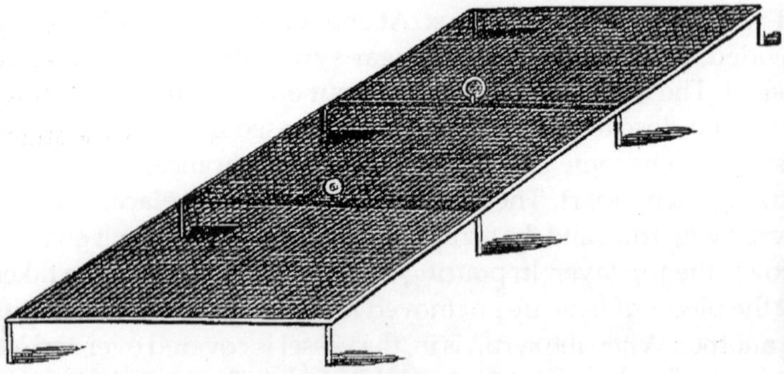

Figure 21

provided with feet about 2 in. high. The rings shown are for the purpose of putting the frame in the trough or removing it. The frames are covered with fruit and laid in the trough, which is then slowly filled with syrup through the funnel. As the sugar reaches the fruit from below, there is no fear of its being moved. When all the fruit is covered, the trough is covered over till the candying is finished. This takes a somewhat longer time in this large wooden trough than it does in small iron ones, but the candying is far finer and more uniform, and various kinds of fruit can be candied together, by putting the most juicy ones on the lowest frame. The drier fruits, which require less time, can then be removed when finished, without disturbing the others which are not yet quite finished.

We generally use a syrup boiled to the thread degree, and pour it straight into the candying trough as soon as it has cooled to 60° C., or to 50°C. at the most. The cold trough and its contents then soon bring it to the crystallising point. The subsequent cooling, however, is very slow, so that the syrup will continue to deposit crystals on the fruit for a long time. Hence by leaving the fruit in for a shorter or longer time, any desired thickness of crust can be secured.

The most difficult fruits to candy well are very juicy ones, such as apricots and peaches. These should be first skinned by dipping them for an instant in boiling water, then rubbing the skin off with the fingers. They should also be put on the bottom of the trough, so as to be in the syrup for the longest time. Exceptionally juicy fruits, such as strawberries, raspberries, and mulberries, must not be laid on frames at all, but hung in the syrup so as to touch it on all sides. Orange peel and slices of pine-apples, too, most either be suspended or candied twice over, being turned carefully after the first candying, so that the side which was at first undermost may become candied.

For very juicy fruits the sugar should be boiled to strong thread, so as to get the surface quickly covered with crystals and prevent loss of juice.

If very fine-looking specimens are wanted, of pine-apple for example, they are treated separately at first in syrup boiled to strong thread, and then hung in the larger vessels when they have received a preliminary coating.

In candying very juicy fruit the syrup must be used at as low a temperature as possible, for fear of the fruit becoming wrinkled, and hence suffering in appearance.

A process which is often employed with specially fine fruits is to hang them by a thread or to transfix them with a wire, and then dip them into strongly boiled syrup which has cooled down to about 50° C. They are then sprinkled over with very finely powdered white sugar and hung up. The powdered sugar gradually dissolves in the syrup, and the whole mass sets on the outside of the fruit to a thick transparent varnish. When the fruit is dry enough to form a tough thread when the tip of the finger is applied to them and then removed, they are again hung in syrup boiled to strong thread, until they are thickly crusted with crystals. This laborious process is only carried out with whole pine-apples or peaches of irreproachable appearance. It gives an article of exceptional beauty.

When on the removal of a sample from the uppermost frame of the candying trough it is seen to be ready, the frame is lifted out, and when it has drained into the trough, goes direct with its contents into the drying-room. When all the frames are out, the syrup is run off. This is mixed with one-fourth of the weight of sugar originally employed to make it, and returned to the boiling pan for use over again. The same syrup cannot, however, be used over and over again indefinitely. Every time it is heated some of the sugar is converted into uncrystallisable sugar, and at last enough is formed to make the syrup useless for candying purposes. Besides, the repeated boilings gradually colour the syrup, which becomes unfit for candying for that reason alone.

The best outlet for such altered sugar is to use it for preserves, for which it answers admirably. All that has to be done is to heat it to 65°C., pour it over the fruit, and close the vessel at once. If the syrup has become very dark it can be discolourised with animal-charcoal as before described. The use of these waste syrups from the candying trough for preservation has also the special advantage that they are not apt to crystallise in the storage vessel.

The drying of the candied fruits may be greatly accelerated by dusting them with powdered sugar. The arrangement of the drying-room simply requires a cast-iron jacketed stove to heat air passing through the jacket on its way to the room. Supports are provided inside the room for the frames full of fruit. The room should not be too lofty, or the parts near the ceiling will be difficult of access and will probably be insufficiently warmed. Thus space will be wasted. If the temperature of the drying-room does not exceed 40° C., it can be used, not merely for drying candied fruit, which dries very quickly indeed at that temperature, but for preserving fresh fruit as described. If a drying cupboard only is used, it can be well warmed by a large flower pot full of glowing charcoal having a well-fitting cover, and supplied with air only through the hole in the bottom, which must be kept clear and at some little distance above the floor supports. Such an arrangement is a slow combustion stove, which gives a very uniform heat.

Chapter 49
Caramelised Fruit

It is a very simple matter to coat fruit with caramel. The caramel is allowed to cool when made until a sample fruit dipped into it gets the right coating at once, and then the whole lot is treated without delay. Fine caramel fruits, such as chestnuts, are dipped separately on a ring wrapped with wire. Commoner goods are spitted together on thin pieces of wood for dipping. Caramelised fruit keeps badly, as its hygroscopic qualities make it become damp.

Chapter 50

The Manufacture of Sugar-Sticks, or Barley Sugar

As already mentioned, fused sugar is at first glassy and transparent when cold. The product can be made in different ways, according to the quality required. There is hardly a confectionery article made in so many different forms and qualities, and at so many different prices. Simple sugar-sticks are very cheap articles, but varieties are made of many different colours and with all sorts of flavouring. The sugar-sticks then become bonbons, fruit-sugar, etc. Plain sugar-sticks are made by boiling sugar to the state at caramel and then pouring it from the spout of a vessel on to a flat plate of stone, where it immediately sets into ribbons of semi-circular section. An assistant turns them over immediately, to flatten them, and when they have set sufficiently, twists them spirally together and, finally, rolls the twisted masses on the stone with a board to make them circular. The stick can also be treated with colours, perfumes, and flavourings to enhance its cost.

The sticks, broken up, give a kind of cheap sweet. It is not difficult to give this kind of sugar very pleasing forms, by means of dies and presses. Pieces are thus made spherical or oval, or to imitate the shape of particular fruits. In this last case the sugar is always dyed and flavoured to correspond with the shape given to it.

To give the sugar the necessary plasticity for shaping, it is put on plates heated below with hot water. There are several devices whereby pretty articles can be made from sugar-sticks. For example, seven sticks are coloured differently and twisted into a rope, which is then rolled out, twisted up again, and again rolled out. In this way sticks are made of various coloured parts, which are intertwined in various directions, recalling the famous Murano glass, which is in fact made in pretty much the same way from different coloured glasses.

Chapter 51

Bonbon-Making

By the name bonbon we understand cylindrical, hemispherical, or spherical masses of sugar, coloured, scented, and flavoured in various ways, and closely resembling certain kinds of sugar-sticks. Of late agreeable shapes have been given to bonbons by stamping. Lozenges, as these stamped sweets are called, are coin-like discs, which often bear on one side the name of the sweet, and on the other the name of the maker, his trade mark, or other impression. A good example of these is afforded by the famous English peppermint lozenges.

The commonest form of bonbon is got by simply pouring the perfumed and flavoured syrup from the spout of a vessel on to a flat marble, where the drops set to hemispherical masses. Even a very skilled man cannot make them all the same size. Uniformity of shape and size is only attainable by the use of machinery.

The bonbon preparation is made by boiling sugar to the crack degree and then stirring in the various accessories.

Chapter 52

Fruit-Drops

About forty or fifty years ago the English introduced a special sort of bonbons under the name of fruit-drops. These were a great success on account of their pleasing appearance and the close resemblance of their taste to that of the fruit of which they bore the name. They are made by adding fruit essences to various syrups, and the consumption of them is now enormously great, especially in the United States. They are in taste and appearance the most superior article of their kind. The manufacture is not difficult, but moulds and stamping presses are indispensable. Although the cost of plant is somewhat heavy, it is soon repaid by the large profits made with this class of article.

Rock

Rock consists of cylindrical sticks of various thicknesses, which are broken up into discs. Their surfaces often show pretty designs, which are produced in a special manner. We will illustrate the manufacture by an example.

Let us suppose we have to make a rod with a white core round which three blue and three yellow points make a regular hexagon, the whole being enclosed in a red matrix. We first make exactly seven equal rods of the proper colours by casting the flavoured and coloured syrup in metal moulds, made in halves. These moulds must be warm when the casting is made, so that the sugar does not become too brittle. In continual use they are soon warmed by the syrup. We then set the white rod vertical, and the blue and yellow rods round it also vertical, and at the proper distances from it and from one another. When they are all truly vertical, a metal tube which can be taken in half lengthways is placed upright, so as to enclose them with the white rod exactly in the centre of the tube. The tube is then filled with the red sugar, which binds the seven rods into a single piece with itself. The internal arrangements are then shown in every transverse section of the big stick. The finished stick may be made smaller by heating it very carefully, but not sufficiently to cause any blending of the various parts of its interior, and then put through grooved rollers, so as to increase its length, exactly as is done with iron rods and wire. When the stick gets very long it is cut up and again put through the rollers, which are kept warm all the time. In this way the rods can be got down to two-fifths of an inch in diameter, and yet retain the pattern inside perfectly. The rods are then allowed to cool and chopped into discs with a sharp knife. It is easy to see how a great variety of patterns can be produced by similar methods.

Moulded Fruit-Drops

These generally take the form of imitations of raspberries and strawberries. Rollers mould quicker than presses, but the latter give the better appearance.

For common and medium goods the syrup made as already directed is best moulded with rollers when set, but for the very finest wares, stamping presses should be used, *e.g.*, for strawberry and raspberry drops, because the presses give the proper shape far more clearly, so much so, indeed, that so far as shape is concerned, it is impossible to distinguish the bonbon from the real fruit. When rollers are used, the engraving on the rollers must be exact, and the two rollers must come together in true register. If this is not the case, seams will be produced on the bonbons which will give them a very second-rate appearance.

Chapter 53
The Manufacture of Dragées

The term "dragées" includes a great variety of candies, some made from dried fruits, such as almonds, aniseed, coriander, carraways, etc., by coating them with a suitable substance, and some consisting of candies produced from any bonbon material whatever, but coated in the same way as the dragées of the other kind. Hence dragées are divided into fruit-dragées and bonbon-dragées.

The coating is usually composed of gum tragacanth and sugar, but sometimes of a mixture of starch, gum, and sugar. The coating of the fruit is done in special vessels, called dragée-pans, which consist essentially of a vessel which rotates on an inclined axis, and which can be heated. The fruits and the dragée-preparation being put together into the vessel, the coating is effected by rotating the heated vessel. Dragées made from a bonbon material cannot be coated in this apparatus, as the mass will stand neither the heating nor the shaking. The former would fuse it, and the latter would break it to pieces. The preparation of bonbon-dragées and filled bonbons, including liqueur sweets and many other specialities pf the candy trade, must be done by hand, as only very little help with apparatus is possible.

We have now treated of the theory of candying, for we have only indicated the methods, without considering the special recipes which are in use, and without describing minutely the apparatus used in the manufacture. We find, however, in all well-furnished candy factories certain machines, specially for shaping the goods. The use of machinery in the trade is in every way to be recommended, as it simplifies and cheapens the processes, and at the same time imparts to the confectionery a beauty of appearance which far exceeds anything obtainable by hand-work. Formerly, candies were only produced in very simple forms, but now they can be obtained in a state which, as regards regularity and uniformity of shape and beauty of colour, leaves nothing to be desired, so that they please the eye as much as the sense of taste.

A candy manufacturer who desires to grapple successfully with competition cannot now dispense with machinery, so that it is our duty to speak of it in detail. We may also mention that we use, besides machinery proper, a large number of appliances such as pouring cans, funnels with narrow openings, small moulds, etc., which can be made to contribute greatly to the beauty of the products. These we shall describe at the same time.

Chapter 54

The Machinery and Appliances Used in Candy-Manufacture

Pouring Spoons

In the preparation of sugar-sticks, bonbons, rock, drops, etc., it is a question of bringing definite quantities of molten sugar into special forms, which is usually done with a pouring ladle. The proper shape of this has a hemispherical metal bowl and a wide flat handle well fastened on. The bowl has a spout at one side. This spout should open widely into the interior of the bowl, but should be drawn out to a long channel, so that it is possible to let the contents of the bowl fall either in drops or in a thin stream. The form of the spout is of special importance, as if it is wrong drops of uniform size cannot be obtained. That nothing may drop from the outside of the ladle, it must never be dipped into the boiled sugar, but must be filled from another ladle.

The Pouring Funnel

The use of this requires great skill on the part of the workman, if the bonbons are to be quite round and of uniform size. The pouring funnel may, however, be recommended as a highly practicable substitute for the pouring ladle. As shown in Figure 22, it consists of a tinplate funnel with a wooden rod fitting accurately into the opening. The filled funnel is held upright, and the rod is lifted till enough sugar has run out. It is then pushed down again, and the funnel is moved to the next place where sugar has to be cast. Pouring funnels are made to act automatically, so that the workman has nothing to do but to keep the funnel full and to turn a handle. Not only does the turning of the handle open and close the funnel alternately, but it moves the sheet of tinplate which receives the drops, so that they are uniformly spaced in a row. When the row is finished, the plate is moved by hand so that the action of the machine will form another row of drops parallel to the first, and so on.

Moulds

Many of the finer and larger bonbons are made of special shapes, such as stars, hearts, rings, discs, etc., by moulding. The moulds are either made by forming hollows in starch, or they are permanent ones of wood (or indiarubber). The best results are got, however,

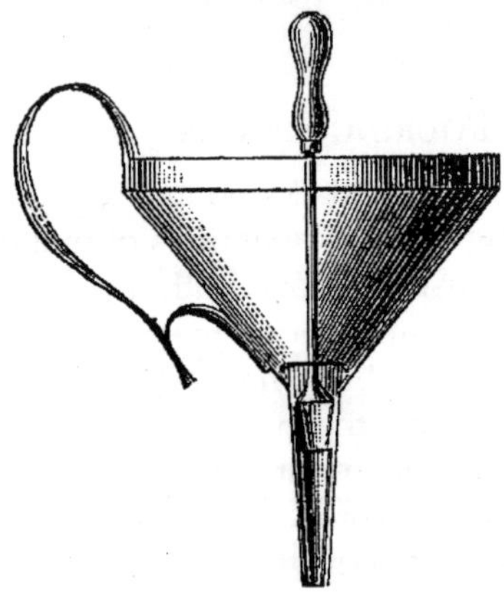

Figure 22

with metal moulds. These are somewhat expensive, but they last practically for ever, and they give a beautiful sharpness of outline. It is best that the mould should be in two pieces. This is indispensable for round bodies, such as imitations of fruits, unless rollers are used, but double moulds, are always advisable, as with them filled bonbons can be made.

The first time a new mould is used, it shows whether it is properly made or not. If the bonbon can be easily removed from it when cold, without damaging any fine edges and without any of the sugar being left behind, the mould will do. Otherwise it is useless, as it wastes time and spoils the products.

The best moulds are those made of bronze. When used they need not be greased inside, as wooden moulds must be. Contact with the cold metal causes the sugar to contract sufficiently to enable it to be easily taken out when set. This quick cooling has, however, two injurious effects. The sweets become very hard, and from the formation of a countless number of tiny sugar crystals, they lose most of their transparency. Neither of these defects is of much importance with second-rate goods. The best kinds of bonbon must, however, melt in the mouth. They are in fact called fondants. They must also be transparent and glassy. These results are only attainable when the sugar cools slowly in the mould. Large crystals then form, which are porous and melt readily in the mouth, and are more transparent than smaller ones. Hence the mould is warmed before being used for fondants. It may also happen that in casing small bonbons, which are quickly thrown out of the mould, the latter get so hot that the bonbons take too long to set. In this case the mould is placed on a wet cloth.

In former days bonbons were made by casting only. They are now largely made by rolling or by stamping machinery. Each kind of machine has special advantages for different kinds of goods.

The Lozenge Knife

The cutting of a sheet of boiled sugar into four-sided pieces of equal size can be readily effected by means of the knife shown in Figure 23. It consists of a wooden cylinder with a handle at each end. One of these handles will screw off to allow of the cutting discs being placed on the cylinder, with rings between them to determine the width of the strips cut. When the handle is screwed on again the

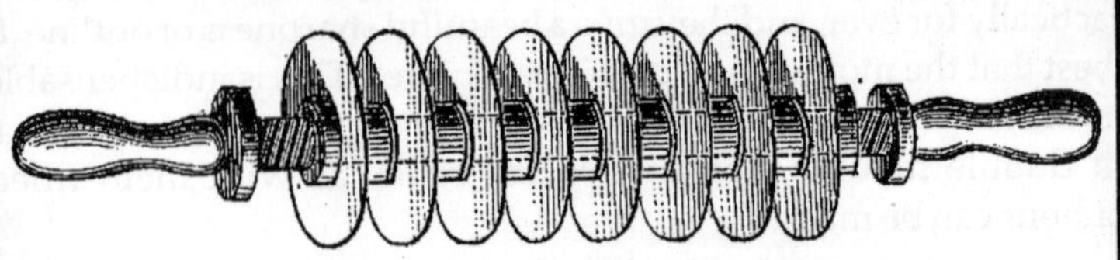

Figure 23

discs and rings are locked in place. By roiling this arrangement over the sheet of sugar it is cut into long strips. The knife is then passed over these again in a different direction, according to the shape (square or rhomboidal) the pieces are to be.

Bonbon Rolling-Mill

This consists, as shown in Figure 24, of two cylinders of equal diameters, about far enough apart to admit a thick sheet of paper. On each cylinder half the mould is engraved. The exact

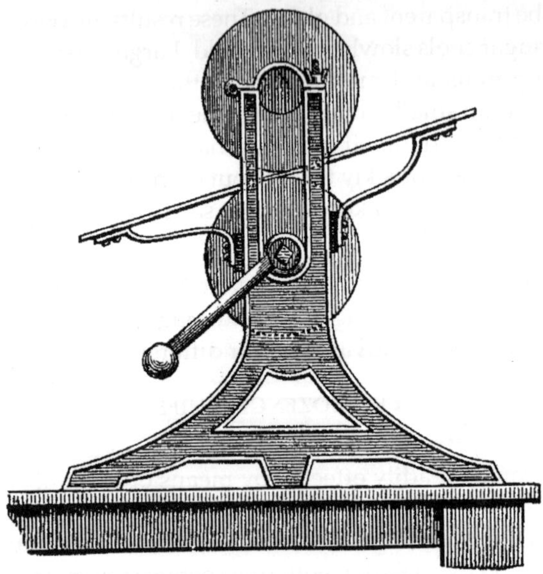

Figure 24

correspondence of the two halves, when the machine is in action, is ensured by gearing the two rollers together with two equal wheels of the same number of teeth. One rotates on the axis of one roller, the other on that of the other. As the wheels have the same number of teeth, the two rollers are so connected by them as to necessarily rotate at the same speed. Behind the rollers, which are turned by a crank, is an inclined wooden or metal plate. On this the sugar is laid in a thin sheet, and from it passes between the rollers. The moulded bonbons are received on a plate in front of the rollers. The closer the rollers are together, the less is the waste. The waste is of course collected and melted up for future mouldings. To enable the bonbons to fall easily and quickly from the rollers, the sheet should be very slightly greased on both sides. This prevents the sugar from sticking to the rollers.

Stamping-Machines

To produce bonbons with sharp outlines, and especially such as have to bear a trade mark or an inscription, stamping-machines are the most suitable. As Figure 25 shows, these consist of an iron stand, in which a screw works up and down. The lever of the screw has heavy balls at either end. The lower end of the screw carries the die. The anvil rests on a thick sheet of indiarubber to make the shock

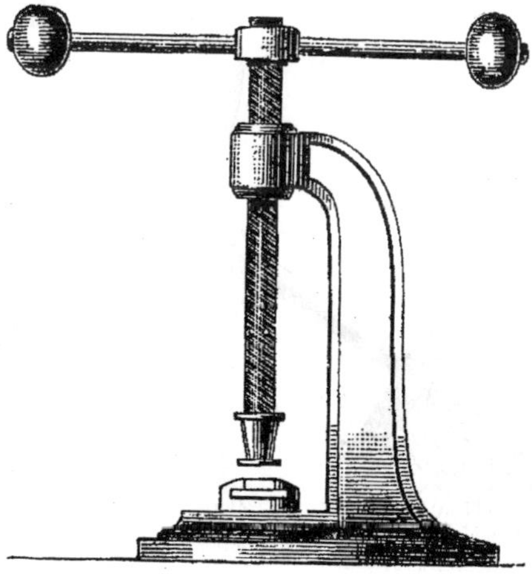

Figure 25

of the descending stamp less abrupt. The anvil bears the die for the under side of the bonbon. A ring surrounds this die, to regulate the thickness of the sweetmeat. The sugar mass to be stamped is rolled out into sheets about twice as thick as the sweetmeat is to be. A skilled workman, can stamp about a hundred bonbons or lozenges a minute with this machine, and they will all be exactly alike. In this way the famous English peppermint lozenges are made. The machine deserves to be more used than is actually the case.

Dragée-Machines

These are special contrivances for coating fruits, such as almonds, uniformly with a dragée-preparation, and to give them a spherical shape at the same time. Their principle is that of the glazing-machine used in gunpowder-making. A rotatory and a rolling motion are combined in a pan, under which a chafing dish is put to keep it hot.

The machine is represented in Figure 26. The copper pan is shaped like a very flattened orange, and is kept slowly rotated on an inclined axis by means of bevel wheels. The coating and the dragées are put together into the pan, the motion of which carries the pieces round and round the sides, and rolls them over and over. The pan

Figure 26

must be kept warm enough to prevent the sugar from getting too thick. At the same time the pan must not be so hot that the sugar is too fluid, or the coating will be unsatisfactory.

Other utensils are used in the trade, such as ladles with the bowl divided into two, and having two spouts, as well as double pouring funnels. These are used for making two different sorts of bonbon at once, using different sugar-preparations in the two compartments. We shall say more of these farther on.

Chapter 55

Dyeing Candies and Bonbons

As all these articles are intended to be eaten, only such dyes must be put into them as are in no way injurious to health. Unfortunately, however, many manufacturers are culpable enough to use, and to publish, recipes directing the use, not only of injurious, but even of very poisonous dyes. Independently of the moral obligations under which every manufacturer of comestibles lies, the use of such dyes makes him justly liable to heavy punishment. The practice is, besides, absolutely gratuitous, for we are acquainted with dyes enough which are absolutely harmless to give us every variety of beautiful colour. As we know by experience that with very many even highly skilled confectioners a knowledge of what dyes may and what dyes may not be used, is the subject in which their knowledge is less than in any other branch of their profession, we offer no apology for going into this matter in detail.

Among whites, lead and zinc whites are the commonest. Both are poisons. The so-called permanent white is harmless, but very heavy. Levigated chalk can be used fearlessly. Besides, the confectioner has a beautifully white substance in starch, which answers every possible requirement as a white colouring matter.

Yellow is often dyed with chrome-yellow or litharge. Both, like all lead compounds, are highly poisonous. As a red, red lead, another poisonous lead compound, is used, and also the heavy and expensive pigment known as cinnabar. Ochres can be used to give a harmless yellow or red to the commoner kinds of sweets.

Among greens we have first chromium compounds. These, however, although harmless, are much too expensive. Then we have various compounds of copper and arsenic, all of which are poisonous, especially the latter. Schweinfurt green contains both copper and arsenic.

Among blues, both Mountain blue and Berlin blue must be classed as very poisonous. Cobalt blue and ultramarine are harmless, but the former will not stand the acid present in fruit sweetmeats, and the latter is too dear.

As we see, there are very few mineral colouring matters that we can use, and those we can have the great drawback that being incapable of solution, they require a great expenditure of time and labour to mix them thoroughly with the sugar. The mineral pigments should therefore be discarded entirely, and only organic dyes should be employed.

We now give a list of colouring matters which are perfectly harmless, which can be readily and quickly mixed thoroughly with the mass, and which will give every colour that can be wanted.

Yellow

Concentrated solution of caramel will give a very fine golden yellow, which gives transparent bonbons a very beautiful appearance. This colour can, it is true, be secured by heating the whole bonbon-preparation, but it is far better to dye with caramel, as else the sugar may be heated too much to subserve its main purpose. Care must be taken in dyeing with caramel, as a very little of it goes a long way. Pure yellow is produced in very beautiful shades by saffron. The dye-liquid is easily made with boiling water, but tincture of saffron is greatly to be preferred, as it can be kept in stock. The saffron should be soaked in about eight times its weight of the strongest S.V.R. for forty-eight hours. The tincture is then poured off, and the digestion resumed with half the quantity of spirit. After two more days the residue is pressed, and the liquid obtained is filtered. It and the two other tinctures are then mixed together and kept in well-stoppered bottles.

When this dye is poured into hot sugar, the alcohol rapidly evaporates and the saffron remains dissolved in the sugar. Any yellow, from the most delicate straw colour to the deepest dark yellow, can be got with saffron tincture, and with the ad-mixture of a pure red any kind of orange hue may be produced.

Other substances which can be used for yellow are the extracts of quercitron or turmeric. The finely powdered material is boiled for at least an hour in from ten to fifteen times its weight of water (soft water is best). The water is then filtered and evaporated to a thin syrup. If this syrup is mixed with about one-fifth of its volume of strong S.V.R. it will keep indefinitely.

Red

Carmine is dear, but redwood extract answers capitally. The extract is made exactly as above described for quercitron or turmeric.

Many of these extracts, especially those of logwood and redwood, can be bought ready made, either in paste or powder form, and only require treatment with spirit after softening them with a very little water. The juice of alkermes (*Phytolacea decandra*) also gives a beautiful red very suitable for sweetmeats.

Blue

The best dye to use is indigocarmine, which can be bought as a dark black-blue paste with a characteristic coppery lustre. The stronger this lustre is the better the indigocarmine. In the paste form the dye is quite permanent, and it affords a substance of very great colouring power. A piece the size of a bean is enough for a whole panful of boiled sugar.

Brown

This rarely used colour is got by again making use of caramel, which is added in the necessary quantity to the water with which the sugar is to be boiled. Caramel will give every shade of brown, from the lightest to one very black.

Green

This is got by mixing indigocarmine with one of the yellows already mentioned. According as the blue or the yellow colour prevails, we get a darker or a lighter green.

Violet

This is produced with indigocarmine and logwood extract. With both greens and violets, the indigocarmine solution is always added to a solution of the other dye until the desired shade is obtained.

Of late we have learnt how to prepare many harmless coal-tar dyes, and most of these are soluble in water. They are kept in the form of concentrated solution in bottles, and are of great colouring power, so that they not only have to be used in very small quantity, but often have to be diluted before adding them to the sugar.

The dyeing of bonbons is largely a matter of taste, but care should nevertheless be taken not to make any contrast between colour and flavour. Thus lemon-flavoured sweets should always be dyed yellow, and so on.

Indigocarmine is sometimes used to give a white colour to sugar that has been turned yellow by unskilful boiling. The indigo is very cautiously added till all colour disappears.

It is of course just as bad to wrap bonbons in paper coloured with poisonous substances as it is to use such substances to dye the bonbons. The makers and dyers of paper know this, and will always supply confectioners with non-injurious paper.

The colours above given will give every colour and every shade that can be required, and that with the greatest beauty, and no others are required by the confectioner for any purpose.

Chapter 56
Essential Oils Used in Candy-Making

Large amounts of essential oils and fruit-essences are used in confectionery to produce agreeable odours and tastes. Whole fruits, too, are used for flavouring, *e.g.* carraways, aniseed, coriander, etc., or parts of fruits, such as orange peel and lemon peel. Besides these natural products many artificial substances are used, fruit-essences, for instance, imitating the tastes of strawberry, raspberry, and pine-apple, and scents, *e.g.* the oils of rose and of the violet.

Unfortunately the finest of the fruit aromas can only be got with fresh fruit, as they will not keep. Every confectioner knows that while sweetmeats made with fresh strawberries really resemble the fruit in taste and odour, those made with the preserved fruit-juice are very inferior. The same is more or less true of all fruits, although some aromas can be preserved better than others. Pine-apple aroma, for example, lasts a long time. In many cases, too, it is impossible to transfer the aroma from the natural product to confectionery. Hence nothing is left but to use artificial essences. If, for example, we want a sweetmeat with the odour of violets, the best we can do with the natural products is to take orris-root powder and mix it with the goods, although the smell of violets is very different from that of the root of the iris.

The best plan of all is of course to use the fresh juice of the fruit. This can, however, only be done during a portion of the year, and for the most expensive kinds of confectionery.

Fortunately, then, we have a whole series of artificial fruit-essences of very agreeable qualities. In some cases it is only possible to detect that a fruit-essence has been used by comparing the flavour at once with that of the fresh fruit. With a fresh pine-apple at hand, for example, it is easy to detect artificial essence of pine-apple, but with the best essence any remembrance of the real flavour is insufficient.

As the use of the artificial essences is very great, and is increasing among confectioners, we must consider the subject carefully.

Aromatised Waters

In the preparation of essential oils from real fruits and flowers we always obtain with the oil a quantity of water, which contains some of the oil in solution, and has therefore a very agreeable smell. These aromatised waters are very advantageous for the manufacture of very fine bonbons and jellies. It is only necessary to pour some of the water on to the boiled sugar after it has cooled to a certain point, to enable pleasantly scented bonbons to be afterwards made from the sugar. Such bonbons are always coloured the same colour as the fruit or flower from which the aromatised water was made.

The waters most commonly used are rose water and orange-flower water. Both of these are used in pharmacy. In buying them the confectioner must see that he gets them fresh, as the scent is lost on keeping. If it is necessary to store these waters, they must be kept in the dark and as cool as possible, and in air-tight vessels.

It is essential to let boiled sugar cool, as far as is consistent with its subsequent working-up, before any aromatised water or essential oil is added to it, so that the amount of scent or flavour lost by evaporation, due to the heat of the sugar, may be no greater than is unavoidable.

The Essential Oils

These oils are abundant in commerce, and are distinguished from the fatty oils by being volatile. They all have a pleasant smell.

Many of them are used in confectionery, frequently in the natural substance containing them, such as orange and lemon peel, cinnamon, aniseed, carraways, coriander, etc. Nevertheless, if these are only required for flavouring purposes, the largest part of them is only a make weight. They are generally used by boiling them in the sugar, which then absorbs the essential oil. It is in most cases far better to add the essential oils themselves to the sugar. By so doing the nuisance of the waste part of the vegetable product is avoided, and the strength of the flavouring can be far better regulated. The ethereal oils are always used in solution in spirit for confectionery purposes. These solutions are known as tinctures, and will now be described.

Tinctures

These can be prepared in many ways, either from the plant itself or from the essential oil. In order to be able to regulate the flavouring of the confectionery, it is indispensable always to make the tincture with the same proportions of plant and spirit so as to get the tincture of a constant strength. We use glass flasks provided with good well-fitting corks for preparing tinctures. If the precaution of choosing good corks is omitted, there will be much loss of expensive spirit by evaporation.

The vegetable matter is broken small and digested with the spirit in the flask in a warm place, shaking every day. After ten days or a fortnight the tincture is poured off, and the residue is rinsed with spirit and the rinsings added to the rest.

Special treatment is necessary for fruits and seeds. In dry fruits, such as aniseed, carraway, fennel, and coriander, the inner parts of the seeds are free from essential oil, which occurs in the husk only. They must be crushed before being put into the spirit. Cinnamon and orris-root are bruised to a very fine powder, and vanilla is cut up as small as possible with scissors.

Although the oils of lemon and orange-peel are common enough, the manufacturing confectioner can often make the tinctures himself from the fresh fruit, because he uses the fruit in his business for other purposes. Lemon-juice is largely used in bonbon-making, and orange cuttings are often candied. In both cases the peer is a waste product, which may very well be utilised for tincture-making. If, however, we use the peel just as it comes from the fruit, we should certainly get the essential oil, but with it a number of other things, which would not always bring a pleasant taste into the confectionery. Orange and lemon peel consist of a yellow leathery exterior lined with a white porous skin. The former alone contains the oil in special receptacles. The white skin contains no oil, but does contain bitter principles soluble in alcohol. Hence the white skin must be removed with a sharp knife, and not put into the spirit. We append recipes for making some of the most important confectionery tinctures, distinguishing those made direct from the plant (Class A) from those made from the essential oils (Class B). The former are always superior to the latter. They should invariably be made from fresh plants, as dried plants yield distinctly inferior tinctures.

Class A

1. Aniseed	Crushed aniseed	3 lb.
	Spirit	20 lb.
2. Angelica	Angelica root	3 lb.
	Spirit	20 lb.
3. Valerian	Valerian root	12 lb.
(*V. officinalis*)	Spirit	50 lb.
4. Basil	Basil leaves	4–6 lb.
	Spirit	10 lb.
	(4 lb. of fresh, 6 lb. of dry leaves)	
5. Bergamot	Bergamot peel	5 lb.
	Spirit	20 lb.
6. Calamus	Calamus root	2 lb.
	Spirit	10 lb.
7. Cardamom	Cardamoms	5–6 lb.
	Spirit	100 lb.
8. Cassia	Cassia	2 lb.
	Spirit	20 lb.
9. Lemon	Fresh lemon peel	100–160 pieces
	Spirit	20 lb.
10. Cocoa	Cocoa	2 lb.
	Spirit	10 lb.

The cocoa is first roasted, freed from the shell, and crushed and freed from oil by hot pressing.

11. Curaçoa	Curaçoa orange peel	3 lb.
	Spirit	10 lb.

Choose fresh peel, which is much richer in oil than old samples.

12. Cumarin (see Tonka beans)

13. Fennel	Crushed fennel	3 lb.
	Spirit	20 lb.
14. Orris	Powdered orris-root	5–6 lb.
	Spirit	100 lb.
15. Coffee	Roasted coffee	2 lb.
	Spirit	5 lb.
16. Mint	Mint, fresh or dry	2–3 lb.
	Spirit	20 lb.
17. Carraway	Crushed carraway	2 lb.
	Spirit	20 lb.
18. Lavender	Dry lavender	2 lb.
	Spirit	20 lb.
19. Mace	Mace	8 lb.
	Spirit	100 lb.
20. Melissa	Melissa	2 lb.
	Spirit	10 lb.
21. Nutmeg	Crushed nutmeg	2 lb.
	Spirit	20 lb.
22. Cloves	Cloves	3 lb.
	Spirit	20 lb.
23. Peppermint	Peppermint, fresh	2 lb.
	Peppermint or dry	3 lb.
	Spirit	10 lb.
24. Pomegranate	Fresh orange peel	2 lb.
	Spirit	5 lb.
25. Rose	Salted rose leaves	2 lb.
	Spirit	10 lb.
26. Rosemary	Rosemary	3–4 lb.
	Spirit	20 lb.
27. Sage	Sage	5–7 lb.
	Spirit	20 lb.

28. Celery .... Crushed seeds .... 4–5 lb.
    Spirit .... 20 lb.
29. Star-anise .... Star-anise .... 3 lb.
    Spirit .... 20 lb.
30. Thyme .... Thyme .... 5–6 lb.
    Spirit .... 20 lb.
31. Tonka bean .... Crushed beans .... 2 lb.
    Spirit .... 20 lb.

This specially agreeable scent resembles cumarin and wood ruff in odour. Cumarin is the odoriferous principle in these three, and in many other plants.

32. Vanilla .... Chopped vanilla .... 2 lb.
    Spirit .... 200 lb.
33. Violet (see No. 14)
34. Woodruff .... Fresh herb .... 5 lb.
    Spirit .... 20 lb.
35. Cinnamon .... Ceylon cinnamon .... 2 lb.
    Spirit .... 20 lb.

Class B

1. Aniseed oil .... 2 oz.
   Spirit .... 500 oz.
2. Bergamot oil .... 2 oz.
   Spirit .... 500 oz.
3. Rectified real oil of bitter almonds .... 3 oz.
   Spirit .... 200 oz.

Remember that unrectified oil of bitter almonds is very poisonous.

4. Calamus oil .... 3 oz.
   Spirit .... 400 oz.
5. Cassia oil .... 7 oz.
   Spirit .... 500 oz.
6. Lemon oil .... 2 oz.
   Spirit .... 200 oz.

7. Coriander oil .... 3 oz.
   Spirit .... 250 oz.
8. Fennel oil .... 9 oz.
   Spirit .... 1000 oz.
9. Carraway oil .... 8 oz.
   Spirit .... 1000 oz.
10. Mint oil .... 7 oz.
    Spirit .... 1000 oz.
11. English lavender oil .... 3 oz.
    Spirit .... 200 oz.
12. Mace oil .... 3 oz.
    Spirit .... 500 oz.
13. Melissa oil .... 3 oz.
    Spirit .... 500 oz.
14. Nutmeg oil .... 3 oz.
    Spirit .... 500 oz.
15. Clove oil .... 3 oz.
    Spirit .... 500 oz.
16. Orange flower oil .... 3 oz.
    Spirit .... 500 oz.
17. Orange peel oil .... 2 oz.
    Spirit .... 200 oz.
18. English peppermint oil .... 3 oz.
    Spirit .... 200 oz.
19. Rose oil .... 5 oz.
    Spirit .... 1000 oz.
20. Rosemary oil .... 2 oz.
    Spirit .... 100 oz.
21. Sage oil .... 3 oz.
    Spirit .... 500 oz.
22. Celery oil .... 3 oz.
    Spirit .... 500 oz.
23. Star-anise oil .... 3 oz.
    Spirit .... 500 oz.

24. Vanilline .... 2 oz.
    Spirit .... 1000 oz.
25. Ceylon cinnamon oil .... 5 oz.
    Spirit .... 1000 oz.

To use a tincture of either of these classes for bonbons it is simply necessary to mix the tincture with the sufficiently cooled sugar. The amount to use must be determined by trial.

Chapter 57

Fruit-Essences

These are chemical products which have a pronounced and for the most part pleasant smell. They are now very largely used, even for ices. Pine-apple ices, far example, are rarely made from real pine-apple.

It is very difficult or even impossible to make fruit-drops with genuine fruit-juice, because in order to get a sufficiently strong taste of the fruit such a quantity of juice would be required that the sweetmeats would never set properly. This is especially the case with sugar-sticks which are required to have an ornamental cross-section. Hence in these branches of confectionery we rely exclusively on fruit-essences, small quantities of which will give a very powerful flavour. For stamped bonbons they are less used, although they answer for them very well indeed. As the sugar must contain a fair amount of water before it can be stamped, care must be taken not to boil it too much.

Many of the fruit-essences sold by the chemical manufacturers are rather dear, so that it is advisable for confectioners who use them in large quantities to prepare their own, or at least such as can be made without a special knowledge of chemistry. Many can be easily prepared with the apparatus shown in Figure 27. *A* is a glass retort,

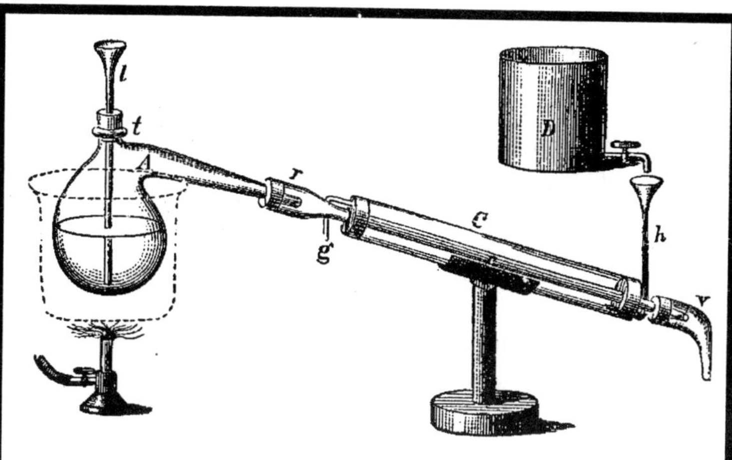

Figure 27

with a tubulus at *t*. Into this is fitted, by means of a one-hole cork, the thistle funnel *l*, or an all-glass thermometer, reaching nearly to the bottom of the retort. The retort can be heated either with a naked flame or by means of the water-bath denoted by the dotted lines. The neck of the retort is connected by means of a cork with the inner tube *r*, of the Liebig's condenser *C*. The outer tube of this is kept supplied at its lower end with cold water issuing from *D*, entering by the funnel *h*, and leaving at *g*. The distillate is led into the receiver by the adapter *v*. The supply of water to the condenser is regulated by the tap of *D*, so that enough is supplied for complete condensation and no more. The same apparatus will serve for making or rectifying fruit-essences.

Before we pass on to the preparation of those essences which the confectioner can prepare himself with advantage, we will mention the properties of those chiefly used.

ACETIC ETHER

This is a colourless mobile liquid of agreeable odour resembling that of fermented apples and of certain kinds of red wine. It boils at 74° C., and its S.G. is 0.907.

PINE-APPLE ETHER

This is a colourless mobile very inflammable liquid, boiling at 119°C. Its taste is sweet, and its smell, though very penetrating, is very agreeable in small quantities, and closely resembles that of the genuine fruit. The specific gravity is 0.901.

Apple Ether

This is also a colourless liquid, but of less S.G. (0.894). It boils at 133° C. Its scent is like that of the finest apples.

Pear Ether

This has a much higher boiling point (196° C.).

Strawberry and raspberry essences are also very largely used. These essences are salts of alcoholic radicles, and are often called compound ethers. Acetic ether is acetate of ethyl, and pear ether is valerate of amyl.

The Manufacture of Fruit-Essences

One way of making essences is to heat sulphuric acid with a salt and an alcohol so chosen that the alcohol will provide the base of the ethereal salt, *i.e.* the alcohol radicle, and the salt the acid to combine with it. Another way is to heat an alcohol with sulphuric acid and bichromate of potash.

Acetic ether is prepared by placing in the retort 10 oz. of concentrated sulphuric acid, 5 oz. of 90 per cent S.V.R., and 9 oz. of dry sodium acetate. The retort is then carefully heated till no more vapour passes over. The distillate must be purified by redistillation, and collecting by itself the distillate which comes over between 72° and 76° C. This is the pure acetic ether. In the case of all fruit-essences the first distillate is contaminated with other and less agreeably smelling bodies, so that rectification is always necessary. In that process only that portion of the distillate which comes off at temperatures close to the boiling point of the essence required is collected.

Pine-Apple Ether

This is in chemical language *ethyl butyrate.* The sodium butyrate used in its preparation is made by melting butter with caustic soda lye and boiling the mixture. As only the fatty acids are wanted out of the butter, rancid butter will answer quite well. Margarine, however, cannot be used, as it contains no butyric acid. The soap obtained as above directed is allowed to cool, and while cooling is mixed with a little spirit to keep it liquid. Care must be taken that the saponification is complete and that no oily drops are left in the liquid. The amount of alcohol required is about half the weight of the soap. The alcoholic soap is then placed in the retort, and when it is warm a mixture of spirit with twice its weight of sulphuric acid is added, a little at a time, through the funnel *l* (Figure 27). The distillation is continued as long as a distillate comes over between 125° and 130° C. The rectification temperature is 119° C.

Apple Ether

This is best purchased, as the process, which consists in distilling alcohol with sulphuric acid and sodium valerate, gives a distillate containing large amounts of free valeric acid, the rectification of which requires chemical skill and experience.

Pear Ether

This is prepared by making a concentrated aqueous solution of bichromate of potash, which is distilled with a mixture of potato fusel oil and sulphuric acid, added a little at a time, through the funnel *l*. The proportions are:

Bichromate	40 oz.
Water	36 oz.
Potato fusel oil	11 oz.
Sulphuric acid	50 oz.

The mixture of fusel oil and acid must be run in cautiously, as the action is very vigorous and develops much heat. No external heat is applied till all the acid is in the retort. The rectified ether much resembles apple ether in taste, but the odour is nearer that of a pear.

Strawberry essence is made by mixing acetic ether with half its volume of acetate of amyl. Raspberry essence is another mixture.

Dilution is necessary to make the smell of the fruit-essences agreeable.

The flavouring liquid is made by dissolving them in spirit. The mixing of different essences and the flavouring of sugar must be carefully controlled by frequent tasting. It is a good plan to make the tincture into a paste with powdered sugar. This paste is then added to the boiled sugar to be flavoured, with incessant and thorough stirring, and a little at a time, until the right flavour has been reached.

We have only been able to devote a small amount of space to this part of our subject, and have had to confine ourselves exclusively to the essences most necessary to the confectioner. It is, however, obvious that an extended knowledge of this part of the subject must be very useful to any confectioner. This he can obtain from Dr. Askison's excellent works on *Perfumery Manufacture* and *Essential Oil Manufacture,* and from Gaber's *Liqueur Manufacture.* In these books the subject of perfumes and flavourings is exhaustively discussed.

Acetic and Tartaric Acids

These acids are used in certain varieties of bonbons, as the acid taste they impart helps to bring the taste of the sweetmeat still closer to that of the fresh fruit. Care must, however, be taken in buying, for both acids occur with a burnt taste, which makes them quite unsuitable for confectionery purposes. The purest acetic acid on the market is the glacial acid, which has a very powerful odour, and when applied to the skin, blisters it like a hot iron. For confectionery use we dilute it with ten times its weight of pure water.

It must be noted that acetic acid has the property of hindering the setting of jellies. Hence to give jellies an acid taste tartaric acid is used instead. This acid should always be bought in the form of fine crystals, free from any empyreumatic flavour. Solution of tartaric acid should be made fresh when required for use, as it is liable to go mouldy. The solution is generally made of 10 per cent strength.

Chapter 58

The Manufacture of Filled Bonbons, Liqueur Bonbons, and Stamped Lozenges

Filled bonbons, which consist of berry, ring, and bottle shapes filled with liqueurs, are usually cast in two pieces, which are united after filling. For example, half rings are cast in a mould, filled with a thick fruit-juice or jam, and then united and coated with thick syrup and dried.

Liqueur bonbons are cast in the shape of bottles without a bottom and with the neck closed. They are then set upright in the holes of a perforated frame, filled with the liqueur by means of a small pouring funnel, and closed with little discs of sugar gummed at the edges. Filled fruits are made in the same way. A hollow mould is cast, say of a strawberry, in red sugar. This is filled with red syrup flavoured with strawberry ether or its tincture.

These tinctures can be used for various excellent specialities in the bonbon line, which, however, have not yet been very largely manufactured. The manner of their preparation is to mix with the boiled sugar, when it has cooled down to the right point, the proper quantity of dye and essence, and then to punch out of the mass discs about three-quarters of an inch in diameter, with well-rounded edges.

If it is desired to impart a spirituous as well as a fruity flavour, so as to make the article a liqueur bonbon, all that is necessary is to put some strong pure spirit into the sugar, together with the other ingredients.

All these goods soon lose their flavours, as the spirit and the essential oil evaporate, unless they are subjected to a suitable after-treatment. The simplest form of this consists in candying the bonbons by immersing them for a few minutes in quite concentrated syrup which was stirred continually while cooling. The bonbons are then dried by gentle heat. The stirring makes the syrup turbid through crystallisation. When the cold bonbons are dipped in, small crystals form immediately on them. A coating is thus produced which prevents the evaporation either of spirit or fruit-essence.

A coating of gelatine or gum can be used instead of sugar. The bonbons are either dipped in a strong solution of white gum arabic, or else in one of pure gelatine, which is of such a strength that it is liquid at the dipping temperature (40° to 50° C.), but sets when cold. The use of gelatine is to be recommended, and it may be dyed the same colour as the bonbons to be dipped in it. The bonbons are immersed when quite cold for a few seconds on a piece of wire gauze. To coat the bonbons where at first they touch it, the gauze is suddenly immersed a little deeper, and leaves the bonbons behind quite long enough for the gelatine to envelop them completely.

The dried bonbons are covered with a transparent elastic coating of gelatine, which completely protects them from change. Care must be taken that the gelatine does not get too thick. The thickness depends on the strength of the gelatine solution, and the proper strength can be ascertained by trial and recorded as a guide for making the same solution another time.

Gelatine Bonbons

Of late, gelatine capsules containing unpleasant tasting drugs have been introduced. These can, however, be equally well used for pleasant liquids, and for enclosing and protecting dragées and fine bonbons. Properly made capsules are pliable and elastic, and as transparent as glass. They may be colourless or dyed, and are easily made by the following process: A number of iron rods of the diameter which the capsules are to have, are set upright in a board so that they all project the same distance. A solution of gelatine is then made, dyed or undyed, of such a strength that a rod similar to those in the board when dipped in it becomes covered when cold with a coating about as thick as stout cartridge paper. The hot gelatine solution must be strained as clear as possible through a linen filter. When the gelatine is ready, the rods in the board are slightly greased and dipped into the hot gelatine by holding the board in the hands, with the rods below it. After a few seconds' immersion the rods are removed and allowed to drain. The board is then reversed and left for the gelatine to harden. This reversal of the board is done at the right moment, so that the coating of gelatine will not be thickest at the free ends of the rods. The skins of gelatine when fully set are carefully removed from the rods, the free ends of which must be rounded off. The capsules are now ready for filling. After this they are closed either by painting the edge with gelatine solution and then fitting on a little cap made in the same way as the capsule itself, or with a disc of gelatine cut with a warm blunt pair of scissors. Spherical capsules are made by dipping glass or iron balls, fixed on the end of a stick, into the hot gelatine solution, and removing the gelatine while it is still elastic enough to undergo the necessary stretching without rupture. When they are filled the opening is closed with gelatine.

Gelatine bonbons must be kept perfectly dry. In damp air the gelatine swells and gets mouldy. To combat any tendency to mould it is a good plan to make the gelatine solution with water containing a trace of salicylic acid.

Stamped Bonbons or Lozenges

It is possible to stamp even ordinary bonbons with a name or trade mark, but the crystalline nature of the sugar prevents the imprint from being sharp. There is, however, a simple means of making any bonbon-preparation of such a nature that it will take as sharp an impression as a coin.

Boil the sugar with rather more water than usual, dye and flavour and scent it, and let it cool to about 55° C. Then stir in fine starch-powder to a uniform paste. Ball up this paste and put it between rollers so as to make a ribbon of uniform thickness. From this the lozenges are stamped in the machine shown in Figure 25. The whole process must be rapidly carried out, or the paste will get too hard under the stamp, which will then crush the pastilles to pieces.

When dry, the lozenges will have a chalky appearance which is not particularly handsome. Hence they are either lustred with gum solution or dipped for a few minutes in water of 70° to 75° C. This dissolves the starch on the surface, and leaves the lozenges with a handsome lustre and somewhat translucent. The famous English peppermint lozenges are made in this way. As the colour is somewhat weakened by the presence of the starch, the sugar mass must be dyed darker than usual if starch is to be used.

Gum Pastes

It only remains in our description of candies to say a few words about the gum-tragacanth-preparations, which are so extensively used by confectioners.

Gum-tragacanth comes on to the market in fine white pieces, which form a thick sticky solution with water. The paste is made from the gum with sugar and water, sometimes with starch as a fourth ingredient. The tragacanth is damped with water, ground after two days' standing, and then pressed through a linen cloth to separate the coarser pieces. The sifted paste is mixed with from eight to ten times its weight of finely powdered sugar, or of a mixture of that and starch. When a perfectly uniform paste has been kneaded together, it is kept for use in a cool place.

When this paste, which may be dyed if requited, is to be used for dragées, only a very little starch must enter into its composition. But for cake ornaments, which are not meant to be eaten, much more starch is used than sugar. A large percentage of starch makes the paste, if thoroughly mixed, very pliable and easily moulded with the fingers into any shape. The flowers and fruits and other ornaments which we see on cakes, etc., are made of such starch-tragacanth pastes, and these are only very slightly sweet. If the tragacanth paste is to be used or making dragées, much starch is inadmissible, as it prevents the quick melting in the mouth which should characterise these sweets. In this case the mixture can only be made sufficiently plastic by very diligent kneading, and the dragées are prevented from sticking together by dusting them with fine starch powder.

We now pass to a collection of the best and most approved recipes for the making of the various articles alluded to in this and the preceding eighteen chapters, including jams and jellies, on account of their intimate connection with the candies already pointed out.

Chapter 59

Recipes for Jams and Jellies

To avoid repetition, we refer the reader to the fundamental rules laid down in previous pages of this work. Cases will occur which can only be met by special skill, and to guard our readers from risk of spoiling their goods in the making we now give a number of recipes. Some of these are our own, and we have most thoroughly tested all of them, so that we can confidently assert that every confectioner who adheres to them closely will always be able to offer for sale a first-class product, and will be fully protected from all loss by goods spoiling in stock, or being spoilt in their manufacture.

We consider it unnecessary to give special recipes for the preservation of fruit-juices, as the methods have already been sufficiently explained. The amount of sugar to be used is a matter entirely for the preserver, as they can be preserved without any sugar at all. It is true that in the case of very acid fruits, such as gooseberries, sugar must be added, but even here it is only done to disguise the over-acidity of the taste. In fact, the acidity helps the preservation. Such a practice, there fore, as neutralising such fruits with soda is to be absolutely condemned, not merely as giving a foreign taste, but as conducing to fermentation and mouldiness.

Jam and Marmalade Recipes

As in the fruits used for jam-making the proportions of acid, water, and sugar present vary within wide limits, they must be taken into account in the manufacture. It may be laid down as a general rule that the more acid the fruit the more sugar is necessary in the jam. The problem of getting a pleasant combination of sweet and acid tastes can only be solved by the use of the sense of taste. Not only is in excess of acid to be avoided, but also an excess of sugar, which disguises too much the taste of the fruit, and makes the jam become horny or grainy on long keeping by the formation of small but very hard crystals of sugar throughout the mass. Such jam cannot be spread easily, and grates between the teeth as if there were sand in it.

A little experience will soon show when the proper amount of sugar has been exceeded. Place a sample of the jam for a few hours in a dish on ice. If the jam is still smooth at the end of the time, the quantity of sugar is not excessive, but if the jam is grainy there is too much. If this is the case, add a little hot water to the main mass of jam, mix thoroughly, and boil up again.

There are various practical signs showing when a jam has been sufficiently boiled. The simplest and also the best are as follows: Immerse a cold metal spatula in the hot jam, and then lift it out. As long as the jam runs off it quickly, the boiling must be continued. When thick threads descend from the spatula and break, the lower half falling and the upper part contracting, the right point is close at hand, and a sample is taken in a spoon and cooled by dipping the outside of the bowl into cold water. When cold, the mass, if the boiling is finished, has the consistency of butter, and if thrown into water, does not break up, but dissolves slowly.

The constant stirring, which is indispensable in jam- and jelly-making, makes the labour hard and expensive. Much trouble is saved by a simple mechanical stirring arrangement fixed above the pan. It is also advisable not to boil jam over an open fire, for fear of burning it, but always with steam.

To combine the advantages of mechanical stirring with steam heating where there is no boiler, we have designed the apparatus represented in Figure 28, which can be constructed at a very moderate cost.

The pan is jacketed as shown, the jacket W being of strong iron-plate. The inner pan K is of thick copper well tinned inside, and is suspended in W by the flat-iron ring which closes the space between them. W is supplied with water through O, an opening which can be closed with a screw plug. The stirrer R consists of a wooden trellis and is turned by the crank M and the bevel wheels K. The whole stirring arrangement can be removed from the pan. The safety valve V can be so loaded that sugar can be boiled in the pan up to weak crank. Care must be taken that W is strong enough to stand the pressure, and that V does not get jammed, or an explosion may take place. If anything goes wrong with the safety valve the fire must be put out at once, and not relit till the valve is again in working order. All fur must be cleared from W at intervals. To make these intervals as long as possible, the jacket should be supplied with soft water whenever possible.

APPLE JAM

The peeled and cored apples are crushed with a stone pestle and mortar or grated up. If a grater is used, the jam is generally somewhat coloured by iron. The apple mass is boiled with from

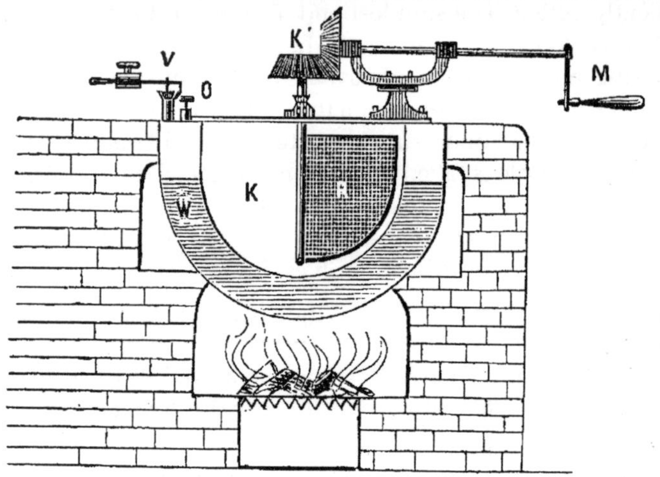

Figure 28

three-quarters to seven-eighths of its weight of sugar and a little water.

Apricot Jam

Remove the stones, and rub the pulp through a sieve to remove the skin, then boil with sugar. Towards the end of the boil a very little carmine solution can be added to give the jam a pretty pink colour.

Lemon Marmalade

The yellow part of the peel is cut up, and as little as possible of the white skill is used. The pulp is cut up and boiled in sugar with the yellow peel and a little yellow dye. If the yellow peel is to be used for another purpose, it is necessary to replace its flavour by adding a little tincture of lemon oil. Great care must be taken to leave out as much as possible of the white skin, or the marmalade will be bitter. To ensure the proper mixing of the essence, it is mixed with icing sugar, which is then stirred into the main mass. The same method is to be recommended for securing the uniform diffusion of all dyes and essential oils.

Strawberry Jam

The little seeds on the outside are removed by rubbing the fruit through a fine horsehair sieve, as they make the jam bitter. It is usual to take equal weights of berries and sugar. If less sugar is used, the fruit paste must be mixed with one-fourth of its weight of raspberry juice, and then kept for an hour at 40° to 50° C. before boiling, or the jam will not have the proper degree of stiffness.

Hip Jam

The hips must be stoned, boiled with water, rubbed through a sieve, and boiled with an equal weight of sugar. The fine red colour of this jam makes it particularly suitable for confectionery ornamentation.

Raspberry Jam

This is rarely made from fresh raspberries alone, as the pulp left of the raspberries which have been used for making raspberry juice is put with them. This pulp is mixed with as much water as it has lost juice, and rubbed through a sieve with the fresh pulp. If only the whole fruit is used, every 4 lb. of it require 5 lb. of sugar; but if the exhausted pulp is used with them, more sugar is needed, or the jam will be deficient in sweetness, because of the water added with the exhausted pulp.

Gooseberry Jam

Red gooseberries are pressed through a sieve, and the pulp is boiled with at least its own weight of sugar, but with rather more water than usual, as this jam has an unusually great tendency to thicken.

Cherry Jam

Stone the cherries (the best to use are the black ones), crush them, boil with water, and then press through a sieve. Boil the pulp with its own weight of sugar.

Orange Marmalade

This is prepared exactly as directed for lemon. If the peel is not put in, add tincture of orange. The orange pulp is sometimes mixed with half its weight of apple pulp.

Peach Jam

Stone the peaches, which must not be too ripe, rub through a sieve, and boil with an equal weight of sugar. This jam has a slightly bitter taste.

Plum Jam

Take plums fully ripe, peel and stone them. The peeling is much facilitated by a preliminary dip into boiling water. The pulp can then be pressed out in one piece between the thumb and forefinger. Boil with half its weight of sugar.

Quince Jam

Made as directed for apples, but without first peeling the fruit, as it is desirable to include the essential oil of the peel, which is very fragrant, in the jam.

Greengage Jam

Made like plum jam, but with more sugar, namely, 3 lb. to 4 lb. of fruit pulp.

Grape Jam

This is rather thickened grape juice. It is made by crushing green grapes, leaving them a few days in a very cool place, so that they will not ferment, and then pressing through a sieve. The pulp is then mixed with half its weight of sugar and as much thick solution of gelatine as will make a jam-like mass. This jam must not be boiled, or it will loss its flavour, but the pots are carefully heated to 100° C. when full for preservation purposes.

Recipes for Fruit Jellies

The finest fruit jellies are those made without gelatine. Some fruits, however, cannot be made to yield jellies by themselves, but for want of pectin remain liquid. Attempts to concentrate them by heat simply result in the formation of a hard brittle mass. In this case, the juice may be mixed with that of some other fruit which will gelatinise, such as that of gooseberry, strawberry, or raspberry. In the choice of this, however, great care is needed. For example, gooseberry juice, which is very acid, must not be added to the juice of a fruit which is only slightly acid but highly aromatic. Instead, we use raspberry juice, but as little as possible, to keep the raspberry flavour as far as possible in the background. We can also add a liquid got by mixing the residue from which raspberry juice has been pressed with a little water, and, after a quarter of an hour's standing pressing again.

All juices must be quite free from vegetable débris if the jelly is to be clear. To secure this, filtration through thick linen may be resorted to, but the best treatment consists in slow heating to the point of coagulation of the vegetable albumen, which forms a scum on the top, every particle of which must be skimmed off. When there is no further sign of scum, the sugar, etc., can be added. As the fruit jellies are either left undyed or dyed red, the only dye used is carmine when the juice is not red enough of itself. It is to be noted that the pan should never be more than half full, as the boiling mass swells very much. The boiling is continued until a quickly cooled sample sets to a firm elastic transparent jelly.

Imitation fruit jellies are often made, *e.g.* strawberry jelly, by dyeing apple jelly and flavouring it with strawberry essence. Such jellies are of course inferior in taste and aroma to the real thing.

Apple Jelly

Fine aromatic apples are taken and cored, but not peeled, because the aroma is chiefly in the peel. Apples, and also pears and quinces, are boiled soft in water after coring. The juice is then pressed through a sieve, and boiled to a jelly with sugar. The residue on the sieve is usually utilised for jam. The jelly can be given a spicy flavour by putting spice, *e.g.* nutmeg or cloves, into the water in which the apples are boiled.

Pear Jelly

This can only be made from a mixture of apple and pear juice, and it is advisable to add some white gooseberry juice. Pear juice alone will not gelatinise.

Lemon Jelly

This is apple jelly, boiled with lemon juice and peel, and dyed yellow.

Strawberry Jelly

The strawberries are crushed and mixed with half their weight of powdered sugar. The whole is then tied up in a strong linen bag and pressed. The juice is mixed with currant juice, to enable the jelly to set, and boiled in the usual way.

Raspberry and Currant Jellies

Raspberry and currant jellies are the easiest to make. The pulp should be so made that no water needs to be evaporated from it, with a consequent loss of aroma. The jelly is just boiled up for a moment and then moulded. Currant jelly is made in the same way.

Cherry Jelly

This must be enabled to gelatinise by adding currant juice. It is best to pick the sweetest and blackest cherries.

Orange Jelly

Is prepared like lemon jelly, with the substitution of orange peel and juice for those of lemon.

Peach Jelly

The juice of the peeled fruit is generally mixed with apple juice and a little tincture of bitter almond oil, which gives a very pleasant bye-taste to the jelly.

Quince Jelly

This is made like apple jelly.

Recipes for Gelatine Jellies

We need only add to what we have already said on this subject that it is quite unnecessary to use the gelatine in such an expensive form as isinglass, which has no advantage over purified glue. Making an isinglass solution in water, moreover, is troublesome. The use of the easily soluble agar-agar, on the other hand, is to be highly recommended.

A proper gelatine preparation should be colourless and elastic, and with it all possible jellies can be prepared, even those with the flavour of wines and liqueurs. We have, for example, wine jelly, punch jelly, etc.

There is ample scope for varieties of tast , odour, and colour, provided they are made to harmonise with one another. Lemon jelly, for example, must be yellow and acid, and smell of lemons, and violet jelly must have a violet colour, smell like violets, and have a sweetish acid fruity taste.

These jellies are often made by mixing sugar with the fruit peel, specially in the case of oranges and lemons. This is however, a laborious process, and the same result can be got without trouble by using the tinctures. The necessary quality of the tincture is put into a mortar and rubbed up with sugar. The sugar quickly absorbs the essence and dries quickly by the evaporation of the spirit. The sugar is then mixed with the gelatine solution, and is followed with the fruit juice and the dye.

Gelatine jellies are always made by doing all the preliminary preparation of each ingredient separately. The gelatine is heated by itself, and the fruit-juice is heated and clarified apart. Thus we have only clear liquids to mix, whereby the transparency of the jelly is ensured, without any necessity for the tedious work of filtering. The sugar is dissolved in the clear fruit-juice. Any tincture needed is then added, having been first rubbed up with sugar. Then the dye is put in, and lastly the juice is thoroughly mixed with the gelatine solution, which is then at once poured into the moulds to set.

As all gelatine jellies are made in the same way, we can confine our recipes within narrow limits. It is best, when no particular taste is indicated by the name of a jelly, to give it a slightly acid and spirituous taste, by the use of a strong solution of tartaric acid and pure alcohol. We mix the gelatine mass with one-tenth of its volume of the spirit, and put to the mixture half a per cent of its weight of dry tartaric acid in solution. This produces a very agreeable harmony with the sweet of the sugar, and the taste recalls that of wine. For punch and cognac jellies we add with the spirit from 10 to 15 per cent of the particular liquor, and then use about a fifth more tartaric acid, to prevent the strongly spirituous taste from entirely concealing the acid flavour.

Strawberry and Raspberry Jellies

We take a gelatine preparation, which only just sets when cold, and mix it with the sweetened and dyed juice of the fruit. The presence of the juice gives the proper consistency to the jelly. Another way is to use a stronger solution of gelatine, adding essence rubbed up with sugar and red dye, together with a little solution of tartaric acid. If some spirit is also added, these imitations can hardly be distinguished from the genuine articles.

Punch Jelly

Rather thick gelatine is dyed yellow and allowed to set. In the meantime punch essence is prepared by mixing fine rum with an equal volume of very strong tea. Enough sugar is then added to this mixture to make it of the consistency of honey. The rum is first flavoured. For this we use lemon oil, orange oil, pine-apple ether, or other flavouring. The punch essence is then mixed with the still warm gelatine solution, and strong solution of tartaric acid is dropped in until a pleasant sour taste is developed.

Flower Jellies

This name is given to jellies having the odour of various flowers. To make them an aromatic water is added to a thick gelatine solution, such as orange-flower or rose water. The necessary sugar and a little tartaric acid are first dissolved in the aromatic water. Another method is to sweeten and acidify the gelatine, and then to mix it with tincture and a suitable dye.

Wine Jellies

These jellies may be made with wine, or by adding to a gelatine solution about 10 per cent of sugar, and then mixing the sweetened gelatine with from 12 to 18 per cent of its weight of pure alcohol and half a per cent of tartaric acid in solution. The whole is then dyed a wine-yellow. The whole may be flavoured to give the taste of any particular wine. If a little cognac is added, we get the so-called champagne jellies. Sherry jellies are made with sherry and a little caramel tincture.

For *Sulzen* we proceed exactly as for jellies, but we usually make the gelatine solution much thicker, and take especial pains to secure transparency, a property which all good jellies should also have. The taste of the gelatine should always be covered with spirit and acid, using an approximate tincture and tartaric acid. Pure alcohol must also be added, however, as the necessary amount of spirit in the form of tincture would give far too powerful a flavour of the other ingredient of the tincture.

Sulzen should be firm and elastic enough to be cut up into pieces for packing in tinfoil.

To preserve jellies in general which have to be kept in a damp place, we prepare a 1 per cent solution of salicylic acid in nearly absolute alcohol. The jellies are dipped in this for a moment and dried in the air. This is repeated, and the two dippings completely protect the jelly from ferments.

Chapter 60
Recipes for Bonbon-Making

These coloured and flavoured sugar goods are expensive in proportion to the elegance of their shape. The best material for packing them is tinfoil, which can be easily removed even from sticky bonbons. We have now in the market tinfoil in all sorts of brilliant colours, obtained by varnishes containing coal-tar dyes.

Owing to the poisonous nature of some of these dyes, we can only use tinfoil which is unvarnished on one side. For bonbons which have a tendency to become damp and sticky, there is no better packing than tinfoil. Fine malt bonbons, coffee bonbons, and similar articles should always be packed in this way.

Fine bonbons should always be what are called *fondants, i.e.* they should be soft and melt quickly in the mouth. This property is secured by using as much water as possible in boiling the sugar, and by adding a little acetic or tartaric acid. Experience has shown that the public soon tire of bonbons which are simply sweet. The presence of acid, however, and a flavouring enables a much larger quantity to be eaten without the sense of taste being blunted. Care must be taken, however, that the acid taste is not made too pronounced. The acids, especially acetic, have also the effect of making the bonbons retain their transparency longer. Acid should be added to all fruit bonbons, but never to coffee, malt, chocolate, and vanilla bonbons, or the like. The consistency given to the mass depends on whether the bonbons are to be cast, rolled, or stamped.

Bonbons with Pleasant Odours

The dyed and boiled sugar is mixed with the appropriate tincture till the odour is sufficiently developed. The weak spirituous taste introduced by the tincture is not merely harmless, but adds to the agreeableness of the flavour. If, however, it is not wanted, the tincture is added when the boiled sugar is still at a temperature of 70°C., which will drive off the alcohol almost entirely, leaving the essential oil behind.

It is quite unnecessary to give a catalogue of bonbons containing essential oil, as the methods have already been given. We must, however, describe some kinds made without essential oils.

Filled Bonbons

Hollow hemispherical masses are pressed out of any bonbon-preparation, usually a red one, and filled with jam, thick fruit-juice, jelly, or liqueur. The liqueur used must be very thick, or it will dissolve the sugar. The bonbons are then closed with discs of sugar smeared with syrup or thick gum, and dried.

Hygienic Bonbons

These usually contain some drug, such as the santonine or worm bonbons. The preparation of these, however, is the business not of the confectioner but of the pharmacist.

Barberry Bonbons

Boiled and reddened sugar is mixed with enough tartaric acid solution to give a decided but not a disagreeably acid taste.

Lemon Bonbons

These bonbons are prepared, like many others, by using tincture of lemon oil to sugar previously acidulated with tartaric acid and dyed yellow. With rather more acid than usual and an admixture of about 5 per cent (of the weight of the sugar) of saltpetre, we get cooling and thirst-quenching lemon bonbons. If the sugar is boiled with lemon-peel care must be taken not to include any of the white bitter skin.

Combined Bonbons

These contain more than one essence, the whole being worked up into a harmonious compound.

Strawberry Bonbons

These, and apple, pear, pine-apple, and raspberry bonbons, are at the present day made from essences almost exclusively. Then bonbons can also be made by filling a hollow mould of sugar with syrup flavoured with essence.

Marshmallow Bonbons

These are made from the usual sugar preparation and the thick mucilage got by boiling chopped marshmallow roots with water. They are often manufactured in the form of *pâte de guimauve,*[1] by amalgamating mallow juice thickened with a little sugar with starch. The tough paste obtained is rolled out, and after sprinkling it with starch is cut into four-cornered pieces.

Coffee Bonbons

Make a very strong brew of freshly roasted coffee and mix every gallon of it with 20 lb. of sugar, and boil to a preparation which cuts firm when cold. The bonbons are then cast or stamped from it and wrapped in tinfoil.

Caffeine Bonbons

These are made by crushing green coffee beans, boiling them in water, and thickening the decoction with sugar. These bonbons are not dyed. They are superior in flavour to the roasted coffee bonbons if made from a superior quality of bean.

---

1 The author calls this "leather-sugar," in good name, but unknown in England.–Tr.

Milk-Coffee Bonbons

These are prepared like coffee bonbons, except that immediately before the moulding the mass is mixed with sufficient of the best sweet cream to give a pale colour. The cream is first mixed with half its weight of powdered sugar.

Lichen Bonbons

Boil Iceland moss with about thirty times its weight of water. The decoction is boiled down till its volume is one gallon for every pound of moss taken, and each gallon is then mixed with 30 lb. of sugar. These bonbons are a popular remedy for hoarseness.

Orange Bonbons

These are made like lemon bonbons, and dyed orange with red and yellow dyes.

Orange Blossom Bonbons

Boiled sugar ready for casting is mixed with fine orange-flower water until a cooled sample smells distinctly of orange flowers, and then shaped into bonbons, which are usually left undyed. To add a pleasant taste to the agreeable odour, it is very advisable to add a little spirit.

Rose Bonbons

Sugar boiled to crack is mixed with rose water or also with tincture of rose-geranium oil, and dyed red. The rose-geranium oil closely resembles true rose oil, and by far the greater part of the oil put on the market as genuine rose oil is rose-geranium oil. Sandalwood oil also smells like rose oil, but is less to be recommended. The finest rose bonbons are always those made with rose water.

Horse-Radish Bonbons

Horse-radish is scraped and the juice squeezed out, boiled, and after clarification mixed with boiled sugar. Bonbons can be made in the same way from ordinary radishes.

Bonbons de Santé

These are made from various medicinal vegetable extracts, such as those of marshmallow roots, camomile, mullein, etc. They are flavoured with tincture of carraway and aniseed, and dyed green.

Peppermint Bonbons

These and peppermint lozenges are made of an unsurpassable quality in England. The characteristic taste, at first burning and then cooling, depends upon the essential oil, the best kind of which is made in England. To produce peppermint bonbons and lozenges which will compete with the English make, we must therefore use the finest English peppermint oil, and take great care in shaping the sweets. The English article always appears in beautifully stamped discs, which have a whitish appearance owing to the presence of starch.

German makers pay too little attention to shape, and often make pulled bonbons. This they do by allowing the finished bonbon-preparation to cool till it is tough, then pulling it out and rolling it on a table into a long cylinder of the thickness of the little finger. This is broken up when quite cold. The resulting pieces have jagged ends and different lengths, and hence their appearance is highly unsatisfactory. Fine bonbons showed always have an exact shape with rounded edges, a condition of things which can only be produced by stamping.

Vanilla Bonbons

Sugar is boiled to crack and flavoured to taste with tincture of vanilla. The bonbons are usually dyed red or light violet. We can also make these bonbons by boiling chopped vanilla with sugar, but with a very great waste, on account of the evaporation of the vanilline.

Common vanilla bonbons are made from Peru balsam, which, although it has a very pleasant flavour, is not to be compared with genuine vanilla.

Cinnamon Bonbons

These are made by mixing boiled sugar with the tincture, or by boiling the sugar with cinnamon chips, and dyeing it brown.

Candied Bonbons

Bonbons which remain soft when cold are selected for candying. The bonbon preparation is cast into the desired shapes, which are candied in strongly boiled sugar, care being taken not to candy so much as to conceal the shape of the bonbon. Filled and liqueur bonbons can also be candied.

Fondants

Fondants can be made by adding to the sugar as much liqueur as it will bear, and still set on cooling, or by mixing the hot boiled sugar with milk to the same point. Fondants made with milk have always a whitish colour and the consistency of butter. They must always be protected by candying or by a coating of gelatine.

Pralines

By these we understand bonbons encased in chocolate, and they and some other bonbons with special names will bow be described.

Conserve Bonbons

These include a large number of bonbons made with very high-boiled sugar. This sugar is made into a paste with an aromatic water, an ethereal tincture, a fruit-essence, or a genuine fruit-juice. The paste is then cast, but what is in the pan must be continually stirred during the casting, to prevent the formation of large crystals. Shallow moulds of paper are generally employed. When the bonbons are cold, they are turned over and the paper is damped, so that it can be pulled off. A still simpler plan is to use thin sheets of tinplate in which furrows for casting the bonbons have been made. These bonbons must not be stacked, or they will stick to one another.

These bonbons can also be made without boiling, by stirring up powdered sugar with aromatised water into a thick paste. Any dye used is first dissolved in the aromatised water. Or a tincture may be added to the sugar, and then ordinary water with or without dye. The mass is then cast and put in the moulds in the drying-room till the bonbons can be removed.

A special and very nice form of conserve bonbons is made out of dried fruit. Special examples are: almond, hazelnut, and pistachio bonbons. To make these the fruits are crushed to a fine powder in a stone mortar, adding lumps of sugar at intervals. The sugar helps the powdering of the fruit, and becomes intimately mixed with it. The mass can often be shaped by pressing it as it leaves the mortar. If it is to be cast, the proper consistency is given by the addition of water. The bonbons are dried in the drying-room and then lustred by a dip in strong syrup, or in white of egg which has been beaten to a froth. Yet another way of giving them a brilliant lustre is to dust the still damp bonbons with powdered sugar tied up in a linen bag.

Mixing various barks, roots, and spices–they can be got into a sufficiently finely divided state–with sugar is another way of preparing these bonbons. Care must be taken, however, not to use too much of these substances, or the taste will be too strong. Among those suitable for our purpose are: angelica-root, calamus-root, cloves, and cinnamon. If we care to take the trouble to chop orange or lemon peel small enough, it will make excellent conserve bonbons.

A very superior quality of these bonbons is made with cream. We add to the cream, little by little, a mixture of powdered sugar with one-tenth of its weight of starch, till we get a thick paste. This is moulded and dried. These bonbons have very little solidity and are best coated with chocolate.

Fruit-juice conserve bonbons are easily made by mixing the fruit-juice with a suitable quantity of sugar, moulding and drying.

Hardbake

This is nothing more than a conserve bonbon containing various vegetable matters. They are made by cutting almonds, pistachio nuts, hazel nuts, etc., into very thin slices in a machine, placing the slices in hot syrup, adding one or more tinctures after the mass has cooled somewhat, and then casting. A very pretty appearance is produced by colouring the slices different colours before they are put into the syrup. Thus, for example, the almonds may be dyed red, the pistachio nuts green, etc. The mass can also be rolled into sticks, which are broken up when cold. The resultant hardbake is named after the predominant vegetable partner.

Balls (*Plätzchen*)

The name *Plätzchen* is given to bonbons which have been poured on to a plate so as to take the form of flattened spheres. Convenient as this method of casting is, it is not always possible to get uniformity of size in this way, so that it is to the interest of the maker to cast the goods in moulds. We can use thin sheets of tinplate with the moulds stamped in them, and fill them from a pouring ladle or pouring funnel.

To make goods of the finest flavour, and to economise essences as much as possible, we boil and dye the sugar, and let it cool till it begins to set. While the sugar is cooling we rub up the fruit-essence with enough powdered sugar to make a dry mass. This work is best done by two persons, one keeping the pestle going, and the other putting in sugar or essence. The sugar is then ladled into the boiled sugar with uninterrupted stirring. This method of saving loss by evaporation is best whenever alcoholic liquids of any kind are added to boiled sugar.

RUM BALLS

Boiled sugar is dyed brown with caramel, and just before it sets a paste of rum and sugar is added to it. It is then cast at once. Cognac balls are made in the same way but without dye.

RATAFIA BALLS

Ratafias are made with genuine fruit-juices and spirit, with a little sugar. The confectioner can easily make these liqueurs for himself in the following way:

The fruit is crushed and soaked in a mixture of equal volumes of pure 80 per cent spirit and water, and left quite immersed for several months, the longer the better. The liquid is then poured off. The residue is pressed, and the liquid so obtained is added to the other. The spirit now contains the flavouring and odouriferous constituents of the fruits, and by simple addition of sugar becomes a ratafia. For use in *Plätzchen*-making,[1] however, the addition of sugar is unnecessary, but the dye should be added to the ratafia. The ratafias themselves, although they contain the colouring-matter of the fruit, do not contain enough to make the bonbons the proper colour.

LEMON PUNCH BALLS

Dissolve 5 oz. of fresh lemon oil in 500 oz. of Jamaica rum, and add 10 oz. of finely powdered citric acid. This dissolves slowly, and the mass should be frequently stirred. For commoner goods, tartaric may be substituted for the citric acid.

---

[1] It is difficult to find an English synonym for *Plätzchen*, the word we have chosen is perhaps the nearest.–Tr.

ORANGE PUNCH BALLS

Fine Jamaica rum .... 1000 oz.
Fresh orange-peel oil .... 8 oz.
Fresh lemon-peel oil .... 2 oz.
Citric acid .... 20 oz.

PINE-APPLE PUNCH BALLS

Jamaica rum .... 500 oz.
Strong pure spirit .... 500 oz.
Orange-peel oil .... 4 oz.
Lemon-peel oil .... 4 oz.
Pine-apple essence .... 10 oz.
Citric acid .... 20 oz.

Dissolve the three essences in the spirit, and the citric acid in the rum, and then mix. The tinctures of the oils can be used instead of the oils themselves.

MILK PUNCH BALLS

Stir up some fresh sweet cream with a little starch, and mix with the sugar cooling from the boil. Finally add a punch mass, such as those given above, in small portions. The punch mass must be added in this way and order, to prevent the spirit from curdling the milk.

PARTI-COLOURED BALLS IN ONE CAST

Parti-coloured balls which show two, three, or even four sharply divided colours, are made easily enough with a pouring funnel consisting of several compartments, each having its own spout. The rods which close these are connected so that they can all be lifted at once. A differently coloured preparation is put into as many compartments as are wanted. When the funnel is used, they will flow out simultaneously and take equal shares in filling the mould. The effect of the result on the eye is very good, especially as the colours mingle slightly at their edges.

Parti-Coloured Balls in Several Casts

In this case the different colours form separate concentric circles. Here there must be a separate casting of each colour. Balls are first made in coloured sugar having one-third of the diameter which they will have when finished. This is then placed in the middle of a mould having two-thirds of the final diameter of the balls. The space round is then filled with sugar of a second colour. The balls are then finished in the same way, but in a full-sized mould.

These sweets can be made in a greater variety of ways by varying the shape of the inner part. We have no space to mention all the varieties which have been made. What we have already said, however, is quite enough to enable every confectioner to invent new kinds for himself.

These balls, as described, are not very solid, so that considerable care is required in stocking them. Each is wrapped in paper, and paper is placed between every two layers of the pile. For transport they can be packed in sawdust or in rolls, like coins.

Pralines

Pralines are made by working boiled sugar with a spatula till it sets. The mass is then moulded, and usually coated in various ways. For simple pralines the sugar is whitened with starch. Pralines with hazel nut, almond, or pistachio flavour are great favourites. To make them, the vegetable matter is ground fine and mixed with the sugar.

Fruit and liqueur bonbons, and also balls, can be pralined, especially the last two, which thereby acquire greater solidity. Pralines are usually spherical, but the cone is also a much favoured form.

Chocolate Pralines

These are made by dusting any kind of praline with finely-powdered chocolate, and drying. For the chocolate to stick, the dusting must be done while the pralines are still warm. Cocoa mixed with a little vanilla may be used instead of chocolate. If the pralines are to contain chocolate all through, the chocolate is put into the sugar.

Essence Pastes

These are bonbons mixed with thick jam, or, very often, with the residues of fruit-juice pressing. Apple-residue is very often used.

This is dyed, flavoured, and scented. The proportion of sugar to fruit-residue must always be so adjusted that the mass is really a paste when cold. The paste is moulded in discs by filling the inside of iron rings lying on a sheet of iron.

Chapter 61
Dragées

There are two sorts of these sweets, in the first the dragée-preparation is only on the outside, and surrounds a fruit-preparation, in the other the dragée is entirely a dragée-preparation made in the pan shown in Figure 26. Fruit dragées are also called sieve dragées, on account of the great use made of sieves in making them.

SIEVE DRAGÉES

The dragée-preparation is made by mixing gum-tragacanth dry with twelve times its weight of sugar, both of course in the finest powder. The mixture is damped with water and worked till it is a uniform mass, which spins strongly. The dye and flavourings are then added, with a little starch, and the whole is moulded. Large pieces are moulded in the hand, small ones in moulds. Hand moulding is used for cracknels and flower shapes. Spherical dragées are made in a cullender, the openings in which are of the size of the dragées required. The mass is moulded into rolls through the holes. These cylinders are cut up with a sharp knife, and the pieces are dropped into dry starch. When dry they are rolled into shape in the starch, just as pills are made by placing them in a rotating drum, which is half filled with them. They are finally sifted from the dust of starch and dragée debris. This dust is used for more dragées.

Chocolate Dragées

The chocolate- and the dragée-preparation are mixed in the finest powder, and then moulded.

Strawberry Dragées

The dragée-preparation, dyed a pale red and mixed with strawberry essence, is moulded in double moulds, the two parts together giving the shape of a strawberry. On leaving the moulds, the dragées are dried and made of a somewhat darker red on the outside. Any other fruit can be imitated in shape or flavour, or in both, in a similar way.

Coffee Dragées

As strong a decoction of coffee as possible is made. This is mixed with the dragée mass, forming a brown preparation, which is then moulded.

Flower Dragées

The dragée mass is perfumed and dyed, and then moulded. Either its essence or its tincture is used, such as rose-geranium oil for rose dragées, vanilla tincture for heliotrope dragées, etc.

Pan Dragées

These consist of a solid core of a hard fruit, such as coriander, almond, anise, pistachio, etc., covered with dragée-preparation in the pan shown in Figure 26. The almonds, etc., are cleaned from all dust, and are turned in the pan at a temperature such that they almost burn the hand. This high temperature is necessary to prevent the sugar from setting. If it begins to do this, the coating will not be uniform. At first rather weakly boiled sugar is put in, together with a little starch, and dye if required, and the pan is turned rather quickly. When the fruits are fully coated and the sugar has partly set, more dragée mass is put in, and so on till the coating is thick enough. It is of great importance to put in the sugar a little at a time, to prevent the sugar from crusting over the sides of the pan. If this happens, the work must be suspended, the fruits removed, and the crust reduced to syrup with a very little hot water.

Large articles, such as almonds, are more easily treated than small ones, such as coriander seeds. With these special care must be taken to keep them separate. While a workman is gaining experience he should only treat small quantities at a time. It is better to take plenty of time than to spoil the batch.

The dragée-preparation can of course be flavoured and dyed in every imaginable way.

The amount of dragée-preparation required naturally depends on the thickness of the coating. It is usually reckoned at from four-sixths to five-sixths of the weight of the fruit.

Preserved cherries can also be dragéed. They are taken out of the preserving liquid, drained and dried very slightly, so as to get them dry on the outside only. They are then dragéed in the pan. Cloves, bits of nutmeg, calamus, cinnamon, chips of orange or lemon peel, etc., can also be easly dragéed. To dragée filled bonbons, roll them while still damp in starch powder, and then put them in small lots into the pall. They must not be dragéed too hot. Dragéeing in general requires much experience in heat regulation. The chief risk is of over-heating, making the goods so soft that they collect together into lumps.

Appendix

Barley Sugar

This is best prepared by fusing sugar, and when it has cooled enough, drawing it out into a tough ribbon. This is twisted into a rope, rolled into a cylindrical shape, and then broken up. It can of course be flavoured and dyed at will.

Parti-Coloured Icing Sugar

This is largely used for ornamenting candies and chocolates. The sugar is first coarsely powdered, the dust is sifted out, and the small lumps are then sorted into three sizes by means of coarser sieves. The lumps are dyed by shaking them in a vessel, the inside of which is painted with a very thick colouring liquid. The vessel is also moved about to keep the dye from collecting at the bottom. The sugar must never get damp enough to cling together. The differently coloured grains are then mixed together. They can also be perfumed by putting tinctures or essential oils with the dye. The grains can then be sold as bonbons, or at any rate the larger ones. The smallest kinds are used for ornamentation only.

Appendix

Index

I

J

K

L

M

P